Wall Street at War

The Secret Struggle for the Global Economy

Alexandra Ouroussoff

polity

First published in 2010 by Polity Press
Reprinted 2010

Polity Press
65 Bridge Street
Cambridge CB2 1UR, UK

Polity Press
350 Main Street
Malden, MA 02148, USA

ISBN-13: 978-0-7456-4417-2
ISBN-13: 978-0-7456-4418-9(pb)

A catalogue record for this book is available from the British Library.

Typeset in 11 on 14 pt Sabon
by Servis Filmsetting Ltd, Stockport, Cheshire
Printed and bound by MPG Books Group, UK

The publisher has used its best endeavours to ensure that the URLs for
external websites referred to in this book are correct and active at the time
of going to press. However, the publisher has no responsibility for the
websites and can make no guarantee that a site will remain live or that the
content is or will remain appropriate.

Every effort has been made to trace all copyright holders, but if any have
been inadvertently overlooked the publisher will be pleased to include any
necessary credits in any subsequent reprint or edition.

For further information on Polity, visit our website: www.politybooks.com

Wall Street at War

'I wouldn't buy a book on risk if it was the last fucking book on the planet.'

Ron, Chief Financial Officer of one of the top five commodity extraction companies

Contents

Acknowledgements

It took time to write this book and I accumulated considerable debt to a number of people. First among them are the corporate executives, managers and credit analysts who found time in their busy schedules to discuss the enormous sea changes that have taken place over the past four decades. Through their generosity of spirit, this book has come into being.

Throughout the process of writing, I had the support of many friends and colleagues, but the book could not have been written without the intellectual support and encouragement of Michael Garnett, Syeda Khanom and Christina Toren. This book is dedicated to them.

Many other people have commented on earlier versions of the manuscript. Special thanks are due to Eric Hirsch, Ingrid Möhlmann, David Webb, Jean La Fontaine and Heonik Kwon. I would also like to thank Allegra Ouroussoff, Ana Carrigan and Aishling Ryan for their continuing encouragement and advice. And I am grateful to the Institute of Chartered Accountants in England and Wales which, through the auspices of the

London School of Economics, generously funded the first stage of my research from 1998 to 2001.

Introduction

The fieldwork on which the present study is based began in 1999 with an apparently straightforward question: how do people occupying determining positions in the overarching structure of capitalist economy perceive the global economy and their relationship to it? It ended, six years later, with a more fundamental question about consciousness: how can a radical change in capitalist values go unnoticed even by those – or perhaps especially by those – responsible for implementing it? The main problem with which this book is concerned, therefore, is that of how we can come to understand the economic circumstances in which we find ourselves. The struggle to distinguish between myth and reality has already generated many accounts and interpretations. My own approach to analysing political economy is ethnographic, a method that focuses on the perspectives of living individuals as they understand themselves in actual life.

In 1999 I was well aware that, since I first began to study corporate elites in the 1980s, there had been a dramatic and apparently irreversible shift in the global economy in favour of finance. With this in mind, I wanted to ask executives about a new London Stock Exchange requirement which, for the first time, made them formally responsible for identifying their company's risk exposure. As I understood it, there was good reason why executives had not previously been called upon formally to identify risk. Given the material exigencies that pervade productive processes, future conditions are likely to diverge from those that have been anticipated – to such a degree that is is not possible to forecast the future accurately. It is one thing for executives to have a clear vision of their aims and a plan for achieving them; it is quite another for them to know what the future may bring. Yet this is exactly what was now expected.

My question brought me to the heart of a global conflict. Once executives understood I was perplexed by the new requirement, all they wanted to talk about was how investors, suddenly and without warning, had changed the rules of the game. As it turned out, the new stipulation was a symptom of a profound change in values that had already taken place within the investment community. According to executives, until the 1980s the collective judgement of the financial community had been that risk – that is to say, immeasurable uncertainty – was a condition of profit. The idea that management should be expected to assess future liabilities accurately and count them against future earnings growth would have been regarded by previous generations of investors as unrealistic. But a change in consensus among investors has meant that executives now find themselves working under the expectation that unless future losses can be calculated, investment won't happen. The upshot is conflict between investors, who believe their priorities to be inherently rational, and executives in charge of global corporations, who hold the new demands to be impossible to satisfy.

The pressure to assess future loss is most dramatically felt through the institution of the credit rating agencies that analyse companies' viability and present the results of the analysis to the investment community in the form of a rating. Since the 1980s, investors have become increasingly dependent on the ratings for their investment decisions.[1] The rating agencies employ highly skilled statisticians to assess companies' capacity for predictable earnings growth. This assessment relies heavily on a detailed analysis of the risk entailed in a company's strategic priorities and on executives' ability to identify their risk exposure. Companies able to demonstrate their capacity for predictable earnings growth are given an investment grade rating, which means they are deemed by the agency to be safe investments. Because rating agencies apply the same criteria to literally thousands of companies, investors are able to draw comparisons between companies across all sectors and weight their investment strategies according to the risk they wish to bear. Three rating agencies dominate the market: Fitch, Standard & Poor's and Moody's. In spite of their recent failure to foresee the collapse of Lehman Brothers – a collapse which triggered the banking crisis in 2008 – rating agencies continue to play a central role as arbiters of viable enterprises.[2]

---

[1] It would be of considerable interest to do a historical analysis of this shift in value in relation to the rise of the credit rating agencies. What I am concerned with here, however, is the impact of this history.

[2] Textbook accounts of the role of the rating agencies tend to focus on their role in assessing the creditworthiness of particular debt issues: see, for example, Newman et al. (1992), pp. 537–8, and Choudry (2006), pp. 477–81.

The pressure on a corporation to achieve or to maintain an investment grade can hardly be overstated. As described in chapter 1, a high rating not only signals to investors that their money is safe, but also dramatically increases the probability that a company will remain profitable. Hence the pressure on executives to meet the criteria is intense. But they can't. And they don't:

> The concept of capital has become highly political. They [credit analysts] have no idea what they are asking. We cannot accurately assess everything we are expected to assess
>
> (Executive officer, international investment bank)

The implication for the accurate assessment of risk is obvious. This investment banker is saying, very clearly, that the bank cannot produce the data on which accurate assessment depends. In a climate in which banking executives are insisting on paying themselves huge bonuses in the wake of a financial crash which they precipitated, statements like this can easily be interpreted simply as the rationalization of a reluctance or a refusal to look hard at the risks underlying their investment decisions. But fieldwork in a range of economic sectors shows that the expectation that risk can be accurately calculated is new and, moreover, that there are good

Footnote 2. (*cont*)
From this viewpoint, the object of the ratings assessment is debt and the ability of a company to fund that debt. This measure is also assumed to be just one of many sources which shape the perception of the equities markets. But the situation has changed. First, the object of assessment has shifted from a company's ability to fund debt to its ability to generate future earnings growth – a shift which places far greater emphasis on each company's strategic priorities. Second, as equities analysts and investors have become increasingly dependent on the ratings, the ratings have taken on a critical role in shaping market perceptions.

arguments for holding it to be unrealistic, which would explain the banking executive's observation that the concept of capital has become 'highly political'.[3]

From the perspective of the corporate executives among whom I did fieldwork, the new expectations signal the breakdown of a whole framework of values which had underwritten relations between shareholders and corporations for over 200 years. Under this framework, unpredictable contingency is held to be a condition of profit and investors' assessments of future risk, however comprehensive, are understood to be speculative: an estimate of the chances of something happening. This original consensus followed from investors' understanding that a constantly changing environment produced by market competition generates too many new variables for risks to be assigned determinate probabilities. An explicit part of the understanding was that, since executives cannot make a profit without generating immeasurable uncertainty, investors cannot expect a return without risk. For both, productive capital thrived on uncertainty.

Then investors decided that investments no longer had to be speculative and this change broke the vital commonality. The change would have had a far less direct bearing on the activities of companies if the calculations were based merely on historical data and the

---

[3] This first stage of fieldwork took place between 1999 and 2003 in thirteen investment grade corporations in four sectors – pharmaceuticals, extractive industries, manufacturing, high-tech communications – on three continents and, to a more limited extent, two international investment banks. All the companies are listed on the New York, London and, in one case, the Tokyo stock exchanges. In keeping with confidentiality agreements, I refer generically to the economic sector in which the company operates.

analysis of company accounts. But this is not the case. From the standpoint of analysts, predictive accuracy is highly dependent on executives' agreeing to implement strategies that analysts believe will generate predictable uncertainty. The expectation on the part of analysts has, from the perspective of the corporation, introduced a contradiction into the system. To attract investment, capital executives are being asked to apply an investment principle which to their minds has no bearing on the goal of profit. Thus the new expectations have precipitated a breakdown in the cooperative handling of international investment capital and a conflict which has redefined relations between investors and the corporations they own.

The pressures being placed on corporations to operate under the new investment principle, and to provide proof of doing so, is felt right the way through their vast structures, where the experience of employees daily affirms the illegitimacy of the new demands. Hence they are motivated to defend their company's interests and to ensure that the unpredictable contingency generated by their activities does not jeopardize the company's capacity to attract investment capital.

During the first stage of fieldwork, I observed the conflict from the corporate side, where it is clear that executives continue to believe and act on the economic principle that strategic innovation and potential loss go hand in hand. Because executives continue to stick to established principles of capital accumulation and expansion, the direction of international capital flow appears to be largely unaffected. From this perspective, the two camps – corporations and investors – are effectively operating on contradictory principles of capital accumulation and expansion.

Introduction

Not long into my fieldwork in credit rating agencies, however, another very different reality began to impose itself. From the perspective of the credit analysts, what is to corporate executives a fundamental conflict over investment principle takes on a completely different meaning and value.[4] Credit analysts work on entirely different assumptions and consequently envisage the conflict between themselves and executives in quite different terms. From their standpoint, the idea of a struggle over investment principle cannot arise because the assessment criteria are themselves derived from well-established universal principles of capital accumulation and expansion and so the notion that they are seeking to overturn these principles has no bearing on their experience. In their fight for reliable data, they are merely trying to ensure that executives who claim to be meeting their investment criteria are, in fact, doing so. This misperception of what is at stake for executives in itself merits an analysis of the interpretive framework that structures analysts' understanding of the economy because, by ruling out the possibility that the investment principle to which they hold is not universal, it misrepresents as continuity a historical rupture that is transforming the global economic landscape.

Following through the logic of analysts' own perceptions of their relation to the economy, I had little idea at the time of what would unfold as the view from the top slowly came into focus. What transpires is that the value system through which analysts interpret the economy acts as a unifying and reorganizing force.

---

[4] This second stage of fieldwork took place in two credit rating agencies between 2002 and 2004 and then again in 2006.

Whether analysts intend it or not, the new ethos does indeed serve to restructure the flow of international capital. From here, the violence of the rupture experienced by executives can now be seen as a symptom of a much wider dynamic driving the ascendancy of values that are antithetical to the competitive market ideal. Thus the question of consciousness becomes even more acute once we realize that an entirely new objective can be actively pursued even while, without any necessity for dissimulation, it goes unrecognized and unacknowledged.

The Financial Crisis

The question arises of whether the change in value internal to the international financial community and the assumption that risk is now calculable had a bearing on the financial crisis of 2008. It is now widely acknowledged that the near collapse of the banking sector that precipitated the crisis, and the world recession that followed, resulted from the systemic underpricing of risk:

> Roughly every three years, for the last generation, a financial system intended to manage, distribute and control risk has, in fact, been the source of risk – with devastating consequences for workers, consumers and taxpayers.
> (Larry Summers, President Obama's principal economic advisor)[5]

Similarly, in his testimony to the Government Oversight Committee of the House of Representatives in October 2008, Alan Greenspan, formerly chairman of the United States Federal Reserve, said:

---

[5] *Financial Times*, 20 October 2009.

Introduction

In 2005 I raised concerns that the protracted period of underpricing risk, if history was any guide, would have dire consequences. This crisis, however, has turned out to be much broader than anything I could have imagined.[6]

These statements from high-ranking policy-makers unequivocally acknowledge both that the stability of the financial system is dependent on the accurate pricing of risk and that the risk-pricing mechanism failed. Suddenly everyone realized that no one knew how exposed they were. If you control risk, you control stability and, as it turned out, no one was controlling risk.

The question raised by the ethnography presented here is whether the idea that risk is something that can be controlled follows from significant advances in statistical and mathematical techniques, as is widely believed, or whether it emerges from a specific concept of productive capital whose relation to reality is itself highly tenuous. The ethnography suggests that the principles of capital accumulation and expansion on which this new generation of investors has come to rely is based on misplaced metaphysical assumptions about the degree of measurable uncertainty inherent in the economic environment – assumptions contrary to those of their predecessors who took the immeasurable uncertainty generated by market competition to be a constant.

From the perspective presented here, investors' collective commitment to the idea that risk can be accurately measured and controlled emerges from a historical shift in their assumptions about the underlying conditions of capitalism's success. As we shall see, the shift in foundational premises makes the certainty that is now attached

[6] *International Herald Tribune*, 24 October 2008.

to the numbers appear realistic – a state of affairs of which investors themselves are apparently unaware.[7]

If there is something in this argument, then the failure of the risk-pricing mechanism may be rooted in the kind of contingent, historical change that occurs perhaps once or twice in a century, and any remedy will hinge on the capacity of political and economic elites to perceive the shift in metaphysical assumptions defining investors' expectations. Whether this is likely to happen is one of the issues raised by this book.

The hypothesis that the exaggerated faith in the numbers that has contributed to the failure of the risk-pricing mechanism is a relatively new phenomenon that has emerged from a change in foundational premises that delineate the nature of eonomic progress is quite out of step with prevailing explanations.

The press was quick to consolidate around the idea that collapse of the risk-pricing mechanism resulted from a moral failure – a reluctance among executives in charge of financial institutions to properly assess and control the risks they were taking with borrowed money. Outright irresponsibility and fraud have certainly played their part, but an almost exclusive focus on this moral failure has deflected attention from another crucial question: the *basis* of financial and credit analysts' faith in the accuracy of the risk modelling techniques and the possibility that millions of investment decisions, made with the best intentions and the most careful and proper attention to risk, may carry in objective terms far more risk than investors can know.

---

[7] The banking sectors' dependence on the modelling techniques provides another example. See Tett (2009).

The explanation of the cause of the failure of the risk-pricing mechanism in terms of individual irresponsibility is being further consolidated by policy decisions of the United States Government. The response to the failure of the rating agencies, for example, to assess accurately the risk of subprime mortgages and, then again, to predict the collapse of Lehman Brothers which led to the banking crisis of 2008 has focused on irresponsible practices within the agencies and a potential conflict of interest between the rating agencies and the issuers (that is, the companies whose securities they rate); the charge is that, because the agency is employed by the companies it rates, it has an incentive to give them the ratings they want. Legislation designed to correct this apparent structural problem is now being planned.

Some commentors have attempted to deflect attention away from the bad behaviour theory, arguing that the causes of the failure to predict the banking crisis were the result of a lack of competition between credit rating agencies and the fact that only three dominate the market, which, they say, has resulted in too narrow a range of opinion. Yet others want the formal ratings system to be abolished altogether, the implication being that investors have become overdependent on the ratings per se.[8] The point here, however, is that even these more radical views reflect a general reluctance to raise the possibility that an exaggerated faith in the principle that risk can be accurately calculated – a faith that credit analysts share – may underpin the distortions in the risk-pricing mechanism that have had such devastating consequences

---

[8] David Einhorn, 'The Curse of the Triple A', paper presented at the Ira Sohn Research Conference, New York, 27 May 2009.

for the global economy. If this is the case, then the central issue is not the range of opinion but the *basis* of the collective faith in the accuracy of the risk modelling techniques.[9]

Many mainstream economists have contributed to the creation of an apparent consensus and support the idea that risk can be accurately costed. They see the causes of the crisis as cyclical, the result of unavoidable tendencies or forces in the system, which can be analysed after the event but cannot in themselves be avoided. Risk assessment models, they emphasize, were never intended to predict sudden and violent shocks to the system. Economists' continuing faith in the models is based on the assumption that crises, like tsunamis, are sufficiently infrequent to warrant investors' continuing commitment to the accuracy of the risk modelling techniques.[10] The ethnography presented here, however, suggests that their strong faith in the numbers springs from a highly specific concept of productive capital and a concomitant theory of risk which have only recently come to dominate economists' imagination.

As responses to the 2008 crisis now appear to be evolving on the assumption that the prevailing concept of risk is what it always was, the need to examine the evaluative framework defining the concept of productive capital that underpins investors' expectations becomes increasingly urgent. The project of this book is to bring this framework into relief.

---

[9] As I write, CalPERS, the largest public pension fund in the United States, is suing all three credit rating agencies in connection with losses caused by 'wildly inaccurate and unreasonably high' ratings. Their senior financial analyst has maintained that the ratings agencies 'made negligent misrepresentation to the Pension Fund'. The emphasis on negligence serves to affirm the collective judgement that modelling techniques, properly applied, accurately cost risk. *New York Times*, 15 July 2009.

[10] See, for example, Gorton and Metrick, Yale University, 2009.

I
Risk

After just a few days of fieldwork among executives in the corporate sector it became apparent that there had been a radical change in the infrastructure of the global economy. When I first began fieldwork among the corporate elites, investors were not overly concerned about the day-to-day running of companies. But that was in the 1980s, and I had no idea then that I was witnessing the end of an era in which, as long as the company showed a profit, investors tended to trust in executives' ability.

The first indication I had that something was wrong was when Peter, a senior executive of a manufacturing company, refused to see me. I had wanted to discuss with him the impact of a London Stock Exchange requirement which obliged directors, for the first time, to take responsibility for identifying their company's risk exposure.[1] Peter's refusal took me aback. We had

---

[1] The Turnbull Report, 1999. The aim of the rule was to bring regulation into line with the United States guidelines issued in 1992 by the

met several years before and then he had been helpful and generous with his time. I telephoned his secretary a second time to try to discover the reason. She told me he was not interested in speaking to anyone who had anything to do with the new stipulation. I explained I wanted to understand his point of view, however critical, but she assured me I was wasting my time.

A few weeks later I was visiting a subsidiary of this same manufacturing company. Robert, the head of the subsidiary, had been telling me how demands from credit analysts to change the company's priorities were creating tremendous pressures on management across all divisions and in every subsidiary. As an example he told me how his subsidiary now had to provide proof that it was selling off land and buildings. The pressure was on them to sell company property and instead to lease only essential buildings and land. In a company with over 1,000 subsidiaries this switch from ownership to leasing would release enormous amounts of cash that could then be used to finance new investment. At the end of my first week of fieldwork he called me into his office to tell me he had just been in a video conference with 200 heads of subsidiaries across the globe.

The Chief Financial Officer (CFO), Robert said, was in a state of rage over how long it was taking them to make the adjustment. 'When the credit analysts come to

Footnote 1. (*cont*)
Committee of Sponsoring Organisations of the Treadway Commission (COSO; see Calder, 2008) which made it a duty of directors to identify potential risk to the company's future liquidity, capital resources and results of operations. In the United States these same principles were signed into law in 2002 under section 404 of The Sarbanes Oxley Act.

slit my throat', the CFO had said, 'I will have only one thing to say to them – that I have a few throats to slit myself.' Robert was troubled by the threat. He took it seriously. But making the sales took time. He was waiting for the right price.

The CFO of this double A-rated company was reacting to pressure from the credit analysts to provide proof (in the form of receipts, etc.) that the company was carrying out the steps he claimed were being taken to maintain the correct ratio of liquid assets (money or assets which can be converted into money with minimum delay) to future liabilities.

The tremendous pressure on executives to prove to credit analysts that they are maintaining correct ratios is a consequence of the control that rating agencies now exert over transactions in equities securities (shares). Investors depend on the credit rating to assess the amount of risk to their capital so that, to be listed on any one of the international stock exchanges, a company must be rated. Ratings are divided into several categories ranging from triple A, reflecting a strong capital base, to double D, reflecting the weakest. Companies rated triple B and above are considered to have adequate protection against default and are rated investment grade. Credit analysts will not issue an investment grade rating, or allow a company to retain one, unless executives can convince them that the company is capable of generating enough liquid assets to cover its future liabilities. Corporate executives are only too aware of the consequence of being downgraded or, even worse, losing their investment grade rating. A downgrade not only leads to loss of shareholder confidence, it also sets new limits on the amount of capital that can be borrowed for investment purposes and raises the cost of that capital – the interest on loans.

As Frank, the Chief Executive Officer (CEO) of a major corporation in the extractive industries, put it to me:

> The [credit analysts'] basic principle is to drive fear that we are going to lose investor interest.

The assessment process requires that executives defend their strategic decisions by giving a detailed analysis of how they will be financed, and then providing evidence that they are pursuing the strategies they say they are pursuing and not doing something else. Failure to provide proof that agreed strategy is being implemented can lead to a downgrade which can precipitate the negative feedback loop that executives fear would be catastrophic.

Analysts' requirement that executives justify strategy in itself represents a dramatic shift in the relationship between investors and corporations. The threat of a ratings downgrade, implied in a reluctance or refusal to accept analysts' assessment of what consitutes 'sound strategy', in effect, has replaced shareholders' trust in executives' capacity to pursue the most effective strategies on their behalf.

However, from the standpoint of executives, the consolidation of financial interests and the transfer of power in favour of shareholders are not marked primarily by a new lack of trust but rather by the fact that the criteria analysts employ to assess their companies assume a concept of productive capital that is incompatible with the objective requirements of profit.

To understand the contradiction in which executives

have been placed, it is enough to say that, from their standpoint, any strategic pursuit, whether acquiring another company, inventing a new product or forging a new market, generates immeasurable uncertainty from which unavoidable loss may follow:

> The assumption everywhere is that failure of control [of risk] is the central concern of business; that loss is a failure of management, but control of loss is not how you protect profitability
> (Bob, executive, high-tech communications industry)

For the first time, through the institution of the credit rating agencies, shareholders are in a position to insist that executives comply with investment criteria drawn from the assumption that capital earns through avoiding uncertainty. The widely held assumption that analysts' predictions are drawn primarily from historical data, coupled with a shrewd analysis of corporate accounts, bears little relation to the reality. Analysts' faith in their predictive accuracy is heavily dependent on executives' capacity to implement strategies that analysts believe will generate the measurable uncertainty they seek.

According to executives, until the 1980s the investment community and corporations both worked under the assumption that immeasurable uncertainty is intrinsic to innovation – the transformational process that underlies the creation of profit. Whatever else might have divided them, a common assumption was that risk, entailing the possibility of loss, was essential to profit. From the standpoint of executives, the effective functioning of capitalist economy depends on the reciprocal relationship between shareholders, who trust in management's ability to judge the relationship between how much they can produce and how much they should invest, and executives, who rely on shareholders' willingness to invest under conditions of risk.[2] While individual investors will certainly regret any financial loss, they also know that a healthy competitive dynamic depends on their willingness to risk uncertainty for return.

This long-standing synthesis was suddenly and unexpectedly shattered when analysts began to insist that, under conditions defined by them, the right strategies could eliminate unpredictable loss. Out of the blue, investors no longer held risk to be an objectively necessary feature of profit. The problem for executives is that immeasurable uncertainty is the condition through which capital is made productive.

> If you don't take risks, if you confirm the prescience of previous investors, you create no new markets, no new sources of revenue. So companies must take risks, but not just any risks, because if you're not right a fair percentage of the time it will show up on the balance sheet. It used to be the case that companies with a reputation for taking successful risks could take higher risks with each subsequent investment. (George, CEO, manufacturing industry)

> The assumption [that loss can be controlled] undermines development. It means you can't move. It *stops*

---

[2] The claim made here by executives does not accord with classical economic theory which assumes a single perspective, a single interpretation of shareholders' motives: that shareholders risk their money to make a profit and it is a happy coincidence that it also ensures the success of capitalism. Executives themselves, however, make a powerful connection between motive and result. If shareholders weren't willing, capitalism would not function.

development. You have to leave me some room to make mistakes and not judge *before* I do something. If not, I'm no longer an actor, I'm a child. . .. It's the dictatorship of the financial markets, the opposite of the real market economy. (David, CEO, manufacturing industry; his emphasis)

From executives' perspective, the values that now dominate the financial community fail to recognize the connection between sustainable profit and unanticipated loss. Yet, the need to innovate – which underpins the dynamic that makes the whole effective – gives executives no alternative but to generate unpredictable uncertainty, a condition which will not submit to analysts' calculation. The self-evident nature of the contradiction was captured by the observation of one divisional head when he said:

The biggest risk is that we don't succeed, not that things go wrong.
(Alan, executive, pharmaceuticals)

From the standpoint of executives, the corporations' dependence on investors' willingness to invest under conditions of risk is not an accident of history or a failure of due diligence on the part of either executives or shareholders. It is, rather, a simple recognition that any attempt to change the world will generate high levels of uncertainty and give rise to the unexpected. The capitalist dynamic, as understood by CEOs and other senior executives among whom I did fieldwork, is an open indeterminate field shaped by contingency and the response to contingency. Under the model through which, from the standpoint of executives, *legitimate* strategic ambitions are defined and organized – what I will call the

'contingent model' – the relationship between intention and chance is far too complex, too enigmatic, to
be measured in objective terms. Hence, the possibility
of accurate assessments of future outcomes is ruled out
from the start, and uncertainty that underpins even the
most comprehensive calculations is held to be the condition out of which profit is realized. Under the contingent
model, the idea that all investment is inherently speculative, far from being perceived as threatening, creates the
conditions in which a competitive dynamic can flourish
– the presumed function of finance.

Because the connection between profit and immeasurable uncertainty is held to be derived from necessity, it
follows that it cannot simply be done away with on the
whim of a new generation of investors. From executives'
standpoint, the uncertainties that underpin the activities
of the company are drawn from the objective conditions
of capital accumulation and expansion and cannot be
made to conform to analysts' ideal, so that, in as far as
analysts can succeed in imposing their views, they can
only succeed in undermining legitimate pursuits.

It is against this irrational and therefore illegitmate
pressure to produce predictable risk that executives now
have to struggle in order to protect the viability of their
companies. From their standpoint, the success of even
the narrowest strategic ambitions is a consequence of
balancing many thousands of factors, few of which are
easily definable or clearly measurable:

> They [credit analysts] take a very narrow view. They don't
> want to know the hardships, the difficulties, but they have
> never been at the receiving end.
> (John, executive officer, manufacturing industry)

The problem is, they are auditing by result. If a disaster happens it proves you have failed to assess the risk.
(Head of legal department, extractive industry)

Executives are faced with an insoluble contradiction. To protect their company's viability they have no alternative but to continue to generate immeasurable uncertainty, yet an investment grade rating requires that capital is directed along predictable paths. In practice, analysts' insistence that future loss is, in principle, knowable amounts to a form of coercion which executives have no choice but to resist. The contested terrain is the amount of uncertainty inherent in the environment and the perceived relation between intention and outcome. Analysts' conviction that, under conditions defined by them, it is in the power of executives to develop strategies that will ensure measurable uncertainty is, from the standpoint of executives, out of touch with all reality.

Anger at the incoherence of the new orthodoxy lay behind Peter's refusal to talk to me about the new stock exchange requirement. His uncompromising attitude reflected the strength of his opposition. He assumed I was one more in a long line of consultants and academics who had come to appraise the success of a regulation that makes directors responsible for identifying risk to the company's business, rather than to question the inherent rationality of such a prescription. The broad consensus among executives – that those who identify with the new orthodoxy are incapable of subjecting their own assumptions to proper scrutiny – for them makes any attempt at meaningful communication futile.

Executives' frustration and fury at the fact that reality does not concern those whose task it is to assess their company's viability is well illustrated by the following exchange. It was my first meeting with Ron, the CFO of a highly rated corporation that controls market share of a product on which the global economy depends.[3]

Initially misunderstanding the aim of my research, Ron got up from his chair, leaned his 6-foot frame over me, and shouted:

> How did you get in here? I thought my secretary knew better. I wouldn't buy a book on risk if it was the last fucking book on the planet.

Assuming his next sentence would be 'get out of my office', I told him that what I wanted to do was to understand the underlying principles that were causing so much difficulty not only for him but for other CFOs I had been speaking with in other industries. Surprised, he sat down, adopting a conciliatory tone:

> Really? Are you going to publish this?

I told him I would. He asked to see the confidentiality agreement I had signed with the company, insisted on adding a new paragraph to tighten it up, called his secretary to have it sent to Legal and watched while I signed. Then he began to talk. Three hours later, an avuncular arm round my shoulders, he escorted me to the lift, having extracted a promise from me that I would be in touch if I needed any clarification for any reason at any time. This from a man who heads the financial division of a corporation that operates three treasuries on three continents. In three hours we had barely touched the surface.

---

[3] Hypothetical examples of such a product would be rubber or ink.

Ron's outburst displays the logic and the dynamic which translates into the same problem across the globe. For him, any view which takes seriously the proposition that a corporation employing 500,000 to 1 million people worldwide, in a continuing process of initiating multiple strategies from opening up new sources of supply of materials to creating new markets for its products, engaged in production and distribution in perhaps a dozen countries in a range of sectors, can know in advance what its future losses will be, represents a myopic, obsessive, idealistic and fundamentally irrational orthodoxy.[4]

When surrounded by people who share their perspective, executives and managers at all levels openly express their disbelief and anger at the obtuseness of the new demands. They do not accuse analysts of being indifferent to the effects of what they are doing, the problem is that analysts literally do not know what they are doing. Too young to have knowledge of the real world – the stereotypical analyst is in his early to mid-twenties – snow-blinded by their own numerate ability and with a faith in human capacity to differentiate between chance

---

[4] It is surely significant that the size of these companies is such that in not one could I find a director who could tell me how many companies made up the whole. Sometimes, embarrassed by my question, they would hazard a guess. In three corporations, when I asked, the internal auditors printed out the corporate chart, but gave it to me with the proviso that it was not comprehensive. For a time I became fascinated by the fact that no one seemed to know the size of their companies or how they are structured. I would ask executives and managers in the various companies at various points in the corporate hierarchy to draw a chart of the overall structure. There was much overlap between versions but not one actually matched another. This does not imply that strict lines of responsibility do not exist between all the entities, but the notion that senior executives, or executives at any level for that matter, have a clear idea of the overall structure of which they themselves form a part cannot be taken as a given.

and human failure that is naive beyond comprehension, their demands would, if met, play havoc with capital's productive structures.

To ensure the continuous flow of investment capital, executives have therefore introduced specialized strategies and tactics aimed at preserving the fiction that risk is indeed calculable. Whole departments are dedicated to producing data that will ensure analysts' hypothesis does justice to the reality.

Very expensive window dressing

is how one executive in the telecommunications industry summed it up.

An executive in the extractive industries was more blunt:

We used to lie 20 per cent of the time. Now it's 80 per cent.

One of the many paradoxes to have emerged from the shift in investment criteria and the massive intervention of new premises is that stock exchange requirements and recent legislation placing the burden on executives to assess risk actually give management the means to produce 'proof' that risks are being accurately identified and costed. A survey carried out by Standard & Poor's, the largest of the three main rating agencies, found that 65 per cent of US companies that were consulted, favoured maintaining the Sarbanes Oxley Act (2002).[5] While analysts and the press can interpret this to mean executives favour the processes because they help them to anticipate losses, the survey results can be equally

---

[5] Opinion poll conducted at Standard & Poor's Corporate Credit conference in New York, 2005.

interpreted to mean that executives favour the processes because they create the illusion of material evidence that risk is being accurately assessed while simultaneously creating a cloak under which actual risk to capital can be concealed. In other words, the auditable processes are seen as positive because they help to maintain viability in face of powerful contrary pressures.

If this interpretation is correct, the effect of legislation designed to keep shareholders informed about the risk to their capital, far from improving their knowledge, actually serves to disconnect them from the reality. In chapter 5, I describe how the whole culture of the corporation can work to produce the illusion of a consensus between analysts and executives which serves to cover up the reality of conflict and the split dynamic that follows from analysts' misguided assumptions.

Most activity designed to resist the new demands is disguised through the fiction of consensus. However, this fiction can come under enormous strain during meetings between credit analysts and executives – among the most, if not *the* most, important dates in the corporate calendar, dreaded by executives of even the largest corporations.

Analysts routinely interview executives to update their assessments of the calibre of the management. A key test is their ability to justify strategic priorities and explain any anomalies in the data that may appear under questioning. Analysts specializing in the relevant industry come well prepared and executives' ability to perform effectively during these meetings is an important criterion in the rating, and so the pressure on them is intense. Executives claim that analysts are likely to treat discrepancies in the data as a sign of incompetence or a desire to hide losses, while for executives the same inconsistencies follow from their efforts to ensure the company remains viable.

The very memory of a recent meeting with credit analysts was enough to render John, an FEO, apoplectic. At one point he began to shake from head to foot. Concerned, I was on the point of calling out to his secretary when he stood up, shouting, smashing his fist down on the table in front of him:

> They're completely out of touch. They're completely out of touch with reality. The people who now direct the economy have lost all contact with the real world. The distance between them and us is very great.

He paused for a moment to calm himself down and then he added:

> But companies need the investment.

The new force in the economy, created by investors' failure to recognize immeasurable uncertainty as an objectively necessary feature of profit, serves to undermine the principle of growth which executives see as essential not only to the viability of their companies but to the future of the economy as a whole:

> It will be very difficult for this situation to change. The question is can governments hold on to a concept of the economy that is distinct from [that of] the accountants and financial analysts? This is now the question at the heart of our political and economic evolution. I am very pessimistic for the long term. If governments can't come up with an alternative, if financial markets remain kings . . . I don't see a reasonable outcome. It will be extremely difficult to get out of this situation. Perhaps something positive will

happen if we have a huge global crisis like '29. (David, CEO, manufacturing industry)

These questions can be legitimately raised: To what extent is the opposition to the new orthodoxy indicative of integrity, of dignity arising from executives' sense of what is right and wrong? To what extent is the specific form of capitalist enterprise to which they are committed underpinned by a moral commitment to the wider public good?[6]

Since Adam Smith, classical economic theory has taken self-interest to be the unifying principle which makes for the efficient use of resources through which economic progress is achieved. The lack of any strong alternative to this view (also central to Marx's inevitabilist theory of social progress) means that it is perhaps only by default that the hypothesis of self-interest has orientated perception of actual capitalists, what we think they believe about themselves and what we think they believe about others. The assumption made by the classical model of a purely self-interested motive would preclude even the possibility that capitalists see themselves as operating within a complex synthesis whose well-defined principles of cause and effect include moral precepts. The relation between the theoretical ideal and the ideal that exists in the minds of capitalists may yet have to be defined.

Traditionally, anthropology has relied on the classical ideal: the idea that only self-interest can sustain public benefit is held to set capitalist ideology apart from

---

[6] There is, needless to say, no inherent contradiction between a moral orientation to the public good and the institutional ambition to succeed.

other ideologies.[7] The depersonalized and self-interested motive stands in opposition to traditional societies where the conceptual interdependence between persons, far from being depersonalized, contains and transmits moral qualities.

Within this comparative framework, the self-interested, amoral individual has come to designate something unique about capitalist ideologies which denies the moral bonds which unite humans with one another in non-capitalist economies, where bonds of interdependence are concerned with a time-scale far longer than the individual human life. Over 100 years ago, anthropologists conclusively demonstrated that, while self-interest may be a condition of capitalism, it is not a universal human condition.

But, as we have seen, the assumption of an amoral and purely calculative domain in the capitalist case may also be open to question. The clash between two rival forms of capitalist enterprise has provided a framework through which a second hypothesis becomes imaginable and feasible. We can argue that executives' dependence on shareholders' willingness to risk their capital to the cosmos of the market, to trade uncertainty for return, is attributed a positive value because of the relation between this willingness and the wider public good. The investor is virtuous because of his willingness to lose, not because he is a good or a bad investor. From within this synthesis, risk – immeasurable uncertainty – is given a neutral evaluation in contrast to the *willingness* to risk – a free gift – which carries a positive value.

The gesture is reciprocated by executives' commitment

---

[7] Parry and Bloch (1989), 'Introduction'.

to profit, which seals the legitimacy of their actions because of its benign consequences for society as a whole. The social bond is thus created and sustained by a reciprocal relation of the dependency of executives on shareholders' willingness to risk, on the one hand, and shareholders' trust in the capacity of executives to produce profit, on the other. Under this hypothesis, the whole synthesis of capitalist production, distribution and exchange is underpinned by the assumption that common good – not self-interest – leads to the desired ends.

By contrast, the new financial elite is invoking a synthesis which attaches a negative value to risk whereby immeasurable uncertainty is identified with loss and seen as external threat. Hence we have two conflicting theories of productive capital, grounded in different interpretations of the moral value attached to an identical attribute of the world.

It is conceivable that capitalists in both camps are operating within a moral economy that does not define their relation to the economy primarily in terms of self-interest but in terms of an instrumentalist orientation towards profit which, because of its benefit to society, is morally good. The ideal of self-interest may simply deflect attention from the implicit moral quality of transactions experienced by capitalists who may well actually perceive their activities as taking place within a moral sphere concerned with a time-scale longer than the individual life span.[8] From this perspective it is possible

---

[8] If this analysis is correct, then the assumption of self-interest may be nothing but a convention driven by a theory whose presuppositions have never been adequately tested against an alternative hypothesis. The important ethnographic question then becomes: how has the classical ideal come to have such a hold over the collective imagination?

to argue that what executives are experiencing is the collapse of a shared moral economy, the breakdown of an entire system of reciprocal relations on which they believe the long-term survival of the economy and the social order depend.[9]

Each time I spoke with executives about the power of the rating agencies, I was left with the impression that the agencies' control over entrance to the capital markets left executives no choice but to defend their decisions from within the terms of the new orthodoxy. But not only do they have enormous resources at their disposal (including longstanding relationships with the press), they also have history on their side. From Adam Smith to Maynard Keynes, the idea that chance and profit go hand in hand has been a part of the established economic canon.[10] Why then, if executives are so convinced of the legitimacy of their position, does this conflict remain silent? Why is the strength of their opposition not felt outside the corporation? Why has there been no concerted effort to expose analysts' expectations as

---

[9] For the benefit of non-anthropologists, I want to stress that 'moral economy' does not imply that the values that determine transactions are moral in an objective sense or even that those who participate in them see the transactions as intrinsically good. People can and often do find themselves working within a system whose values they have to accommodate but do not share. Moral economy refers to institutional ideals which have developed historically (they are not chosen) and in whose terms individuals have to operate.

[10] 'On the one hand, profit is in fact bound up in economic change (but because change is the condition of uncertainty), and on the other, it is clearly the result of risk, or what good usage calls such, but only of a unique kind of risk, which is not susceptible to measurement' (Knight, 1921, p. 48). Note that my claim here is that the classical economic canon corresponds with executives' ideas, not that these ideas have been proven.

unworkable? Very occasionally, CEOs have expressed their hostility to the new measures. The head of Gillette famously allowed it to be reported that he stood silent in the face of analysts as they made their demands for more data.[11] But isolated public displays provide no indication of the deep division between perceptions of the economy, and the widespread and collective nature of the opposition to analysts' criteria.

I put the question directly to one senior executive. I asked why, given the strength of the disagreement and the resources at their disposal, there has been no co-ordinated and collective challenge.

> Some CEOs are accomplices, most are frightened and so won't express what they really believe because of [their fear of] retribution. If you discuss this in the establishment, even being extremely careful not to attribute blame of any kind, little by little you'll find yourself out of the establishment because they have to believe in it themselves. If you speak clearly and openly about this they will close the doors. (Robert, extractive industries)

Robert's reply confirmed the consolidated atmosphere of acceptance of the credibility of the ratings, but he did not answer my question. While there is always the possibility that executives' collective power is not perceived as a resource, as we shall see in chapter 5, a more likely explanation is that the now-routine manipulation of data leaves them deeply compromised so that the impulse is to protect companies from scrutiny rather

---

[11] 'The End of Myth-making and a Return to True Analysis', *Financial Times*, 22 January 2002.

than to draw attention to problems surrounding their ability to supply what analysts consider to be reliable data. The question driving executives is: how can we count on least interference?

By the end of this first phase of fieldwork I shared executives' views that the lack of a concrete understanding of the real conditions under which profit is made, coupled with an exaggerated belief in their own powers of calculation, had effectively disconnected analysts and the investment community from a rational understanding of risk.

What I found truly remarkable was the apparent incapacity of analysts to see that their insistence that risk is measurable and controllable breaks with established investment principles. Capitalism's sacred cow, the freedom to innovate, to generate immeasurable uncertainty – the one factor, according to free market doctrine, that is supposed to secure capitalism's advancement – appeared to hold little or no value for the new elite.

Naturally, I wanted to know how analysts defended this inconsistency, but, in any case, the exigencies of ethnographic method – 'to treat the beliefs of another man from his point of view' – required I test my understanding against analysts' own perceptions. Thus I was thrust into a world I could not have imagined. The shift to the credit analysts' perspective forced an entirely different world economy into view. Their perspective is the subject of the next three chapters.

2

Certainty

One cannot be aware of what one does not know.

When I began this phase of fieldwork the idea that my perception of the global economy was about to be radically changed was not on the horizon of possibilities. As I came out onto the fifty-seventh floor of one of the three major credit rating agencies, Phil, a director, was there to greet me.

'Would you like a tour?' Phil asked. 'We have one of the best views in Manhattan.'

The corridor opened onto the sea and across the Atlantic Ocean to infinity.

The magnificent view was undercut by a warren of tidy cubicles. Most were empty. Phil, one of several directors, had an office. His secretary offered coffee. He was relaxed, laid-back even. He knew I had just come from fieldwork in a number of corporations that the agency rates. I explained on the telephone that I wanted to talk to him about executive claims that analysts do not understand the meaning of the term 'risk', but to my surprise he showed no curiosity about my findings. I decided to get straight to the point and began by asking how the agencies had come to have so much sway over the global economy. The question seemed to catch him off guard.

> Phil: I think the problem now is we have too much visibility . . . or weight. Perhaps weight is a better description. [Corporate] executives think we are *making* them take decisions. We don't want them to feel that. [His emphasis]
>
> Me: But do you think it is only a question of perception?
>
> Phil: We clearly have had weight in the US for the last thirty years, but agencies did not exist in Europe until '85.
>
> Me: OK. But what would you say *accounts* for the expansion of the [rating] agencies?

There followed an increasingly tense silence. Then Phil said:

> The markets have evolved. It was beneficial for the whole market.

More silence and then, irritably:

> Before it was abnormal, now it is normal – to answer your question.

A few more uncomfortable moments passed before Phil took the initiative and asked whether I had any questions about the method they use to rate corporations. Is this what most journalists and academics want to discuss? I asked.

> Phil: Yes.
>
> Me: The viability of the models [for calculating a rating]?
>
> Phil: Yes. No one has ever asked me a question like *that*.

Phil's reluctance to address my initial question about the increased influence of the credit rating agencies in relation to the global economy as a whole took me by surprise. I had expected him to have a well-rehearsed reply at his disposal. I thought that he would take the power and influence of agencies over the corporations for granted and explain opposition to this in terms of executives' unwillingness to reveal their risk exposure. The idea of agencies having 'too much weight' seemed a strange euphemism for the intense pressure analysts exert on executives to keep to 'sound' strategy. And Phil's hint that executives' claims were the result of a misperception was incomprehensible to me. Whatever the reason for his response, Phil was clearly uncomfortable with this line of enquiry. So, taking his cue, I moved on to method.

A week later, however, Phil telephoned to say he felt he had not answered my initial question adequately and to suggest that we meet during his forthcoming visit to London. This time he opened the discussion with a description of the event which for him explained the rise of the credit rating agencies.

The collapse of the Pennsylvania & Central Railway Company in 1970, then the largest corporate collapse in history, he said, had been the catalyst. For over a decade, Penn Central's management had covered up failed investment strategies and heavy debt, and in June of 1970, with shareholders still believing Penn Central to be solvent, the Company filed for bankruptcy. The intervention of the Nixon Administration (the first government intervention in US history) prevented the economic destabilization of the eastern seaboard.[1]

---

[1] 'The Financial Collapse of the Penn Central Company', Staff report of the Securities and Exchange Commission to the Special Subcommittee on Investigations, Washington, 1972.

According to Phil, shareholders concluded from this that if the executives of one of America's most prestigious corporations could mislead investors into believing that a near-bankrupt company was still profitable, then executives could do it anywhere.

He explained: Until Penn Central the rating agencies didn't have much of a role, there was limited investor participation. Agencies took on a different dimension after Penn Central. It was a traumatic experience for the markets – a watershed event.

As a result, shareholders began to pay closer attention to how executives were investing their money. They wanted to know that they were, in fact, carrying out their stated objectives.

> Phil: This thrust the rating agencies into the heart of the economy. Now all the markets look to the ratings. Now it has become a market convention, a market expectation. Now, if a US investor wanted to invest in Hong Kong or in Berlin, he would be used to having a rating, he would ask for a rating. It creates a demand, it's cumulative, a demand repeating itself thousands of times. When fund managers made a decision that they would request ratings for all their meetings, when they decided that all companies should get ratings, it established a much broader base. Twenty years ago if ICI wanted a rating we had to send someone overseas. We now have offices in nineteen or twenty cities: Stockholm, Buenos Aires, São Paulo.

He listed them, along with the independent rating agencies they had recently bought out.

Phil made no mention of a change in investment criteria. According to him, the ability of the credit rating agencies to make objective, independent assessments of a corporation's future viability simply placed shareholder investment strategy on a more rational footing. Shareholders could now organize their investment portfolios on the basis of knowledge of their risk exposure. As Phil explained, the ratings give shareholders the security of knowing how much risk is tied to their investments.

Phil's history makes sense of the rise of the agencies in terms of shareholders' desire for greater objectivity. He aligns the ascendancy with a rational move by investors towards safer, reliable investment strategies. There is no indication of any discontinuity in investment principle and nothing ambiguous about the idea that the rise of the credit rating agencies has been beneficial to the economy as a whole. On the contrary, the collapse of Penn Central proves that shareholders need the agencies.

My impression at the time – and I still think this is true – was that Phil's explanation for shareholders' increased dependence on the rating agencies was not strategic and he believed what he was saying.[2] However, his portrayal of a smooth transition from what he saw as precarious and unreliable investment strategies to strategies based on sound information suggested a lack

---

[2] Phil's history stumbles on the first test of descriptive accuracy. At the time of its collapse, Penn Central was rated by Moody's as investment grade. In its report on the collapse, the United States Security and Exchange Commission laid considerable blame on the rating agency for misleading shareholders into a sense of false security as to the safety of their investments. The important ethnographic point is that the interpretive framework produces a moral tale which is put forward as history. I would ask the reader not to conclude just yet that I am being naive in my judgement that Phil believes he is being factual. Arguments backing this initial impression will emerge more fully in the discussions in chapters 3 and 6.

of awareness of executive resistance I found difficult to believe. His colleagues also seemed to share his view. The replies of other analysts to the same question – how had the agencies come to have so much influence over the global economy – gave a similar impression of a well-established consensus within the agency:

> Alan: The markets have been reawakened in a big way. Shareholders now want to know you are avoiding risk exposure. Just because a brand is known doesn't mean it is a good investment.

Or:

> Andrea: Yes, this [transition] is as true for the US as for Europe. It happened earlier in the US than Britain.

Or again:

> Otto: The 1970s was a time when financing in general was becoming more globalized. The flow of capital was being liberalized. Investors ceased to be regionally or nationally based. . .they wanted better information.

The implication was of a strong consensus: that everyone (presumably including corporate executives) shared the view that there had been a change in shareholder's expectations and this change amounted to an unambiguous progressive adjustment in favour of both shareholders and the economy as a whole.

For reasons yet to be discovered, the pressure exerted by analysts on executives to revise their investment strategy – which Phil ambiguously referred to as 'too much weight' – was not integrated into the public image of the agency's ascendancy and so, without other information, I would have been left with the over-riding impression that the principle that risk can be accurately assessed is both universal and continuous with the past. This was not the moment to press analysts on a question whose answer they seemed to find self-evident. I put the issue of conflict to one side for the time being and went along with their chosen point of departure.

Numbers bring analysts to life. 'Everything depends on the method', was a phrase often repeated. Method orientates the discussion towards what really excites credit ratings analysts and brings us into the global economy on their terms.

The Method

Triple A is the safest investment with almost no chance of default. A Triple A is 5 per cent risk – virtually risk free. We guarantee 95 per cent risk free. Double B represents 12 per cent default rate. Anything below BB is non-investment grade. (Michel, senior analyst)

Michel's faith in the accuracy of the ratings struck me as truly extraordinary. It sounded to me as though he was guaranteeing the future of the company, i.e. zero risk of failure. I picked him up on this, imagining he would quickly acknowledge this claim to be a bit of hyperbole. But he didn't check me.

Me: But Michel, how can you *guarantee* the future viability of a company? This really has got to be nonsense.

Michel: Everything depends on accuracy. Everything depends on identifying correctly the patterns of expansion and contraction within a given economic sector, on knowing where and when loss will occur. Ideally a model brings in ten years' worth of data while expanding the window and moving forward on the basis of new data. All models undergo constant update and development.[3]

How can people whose work depends on precision speak so confidently in terms of virtually guaranteeing the future viability of a corporation? Analysts are trained in statistics, and statistically a prediction is an *estimate* of the chances of something happening. I said as much to Michel, but he was adamant. The degree of confidence in their assessment, he said, is based on the quality and the quantity of the data from which analysts derive sector trends. Because publicly quoted companies in all sectors of the economy now have to have a rating, agencies have unprecedented access to details of the terms on which thousands of corporations conduct their business. It is the massive increase in the quality of the data that explains their capacity to guarantee the level of risk to capital.

Michel explained that, within the context of these well-supported sector trends, analysts can assess with precision the ratio of each company's accessible capital – cash and assets – to its future liabilities. Analysts say they now know, for example, that a triple A-rated company will continue to generate sufficient revenue to finance its future liabilities while simultaneously increasing earnings growth. Thanks to the sophistication of the assessment techniques and the quality and quantity of the primary data, default rates no longer

---

[3] In formal settings and official documents, analysts are careful only to refer to estimates of the chances of failure and to say that what they are offering shareholders is merely an opinion. However, in spontaneous internal conversation, analysts speak of a guarantee.

represent an estimate of the chances of future loss, but rather, impending known loss.

It was beginning to sound as if analysts believe that immeasurable uncertainty can in principle be eliminated from the economy as a whole. But this is not the case. As one senior credit analyst explained, some sectors operate under conditions of very high uncertainty where the potential for loss cannot be easily measured.

> John: Ratings for the steel industry tend to be very low because so many unpredictable factors influence the market. All risks are controlled, if you listen to management, but things always go wrong, so the rating is low. Only a very small proportion of investors are willing to invest in steel. None of the normal markets want risk.[4]

For corporations operating in conditions of high uncertainty, the claim is precisely this: future unknown. The most important distinction is between corporations whose future viability and earnings growth can be counted on, and corporations whose future losses and earnings are uncertain. This is the distinction between investment and non-investment grade companies.

Fieldwork exclusively in investment grade companies had introduced a bias and misled me into imagining that analysts assumed a determinate world. The first thing analysts look at when assessing a company, however, is their ability to measure the risk, given the conditions in which the company is operating. A company operating in a highly competitive environment with restricted

---

[4] More recently steel production has shifted towards 'vertical integration' and the trend towards controlling production from the raw material to finished product has, according to analysts, significantly lowered uncertainty for this sector.

profit margins will be less likely to be given a high rating than a company projected to have 'solid earnings growth'.

The picture that was beginning to emerge was of an economic domain within which risk exposure can be given a determinate probability and outside of which investment is considered highly speculative. The claim of a calculable future does not apply, as I initially imagined, to the whole economic system: analysts are not claiming a total determinism. Rather, the calculable future applies to a domain of carefully selected 'quality companies' which, according to analysts, the ratings system itself serves to reinforce.

From the standpoint of the rating agency, each newly rated company expands the domain of assured earnings by increasing the body of data from which the underlying distributions of loss are drawn and from which the trend is established. In other words, the ratings serve to widen the field of dynamic stability. Since capital is then raised on the prediction, 'quality companies' – companies that are rated investment grade – will easily attract investment capital. The probability of accurate prediction is considerably strengthened by the continuous flow of capital into the predictive domain. Thus analysts' predictions channel the flow of investment into the domain where a determinate probability has been established, further increasing the probability of accurate prediction. Analysts' faith in their predictions, which from the perspective of the investment grade company suggested a total determinism, in fact applies only to a specific domain of economic activity, which the new investment criteria, based on the avoidance of risk, has brought into being – a state of affairs that analysts see as a good thing.

The reasoning underpinning the use of the term 'guarantee' was now clear. Analysts' confidence in their ability to predict the future (which, without proper context, appears to rest on an exaggerated faith in their own powers of calculation) actually stems, far more reasonably, from the assumed power of the ratings to produce a domain where contingency – the distribution of chances – can be controlled.

Analysts, then, imagine the global economy in terms of a hierarchy of companies divided into two spheres, separated by their relation to the degree of uncertainty they produce. At the top of the hierarchy are quality companies generating predictable uncertainty. At the base are those companies whose future is unknown.

This image of a hierarchy of companies breaks with the conventional image of a multitude of competing companies operating on a level playing field. In this new image, the essential dynamic is not price competition but strategic activity designed to eliminate chance. This is a completely new representation of the capitalist economy which cannot be regarded merely as a further development of competitive market capitalism.

This shift from a dependence on the competitive model to what I will call the 'rationalist model' was affirmed by Edward when I pressed him on the question of analysts' ability to guarantee the future of quality companies. The levels of uncertainty from which sector trends are drawn, he explained, are determined by the strategic choices of the major players:

A change in priorities for a major changes business risk for a whole sector . . . they have a key role in defining international market conditions.

Major players, in other words, are held to have a determining influence on levels of uncertainty for their sector.

Major players are corporations with worldwide integrated strategies that complement one another. For analysts, the ideal corporation is the well-managed 'pure player' – a global company that produces tightly related products whose resources are co-ordinated internationally. According to analysts' calculations, the pure player generates far less uncertainty than the diversified global company with a wide range of products and services. And because levels of uncertainty generated by major players help to determine sector trends, the lower the level of uncertainty, the higher the probability that predictions will be accurate.

The predictive domain, as envisaged by analysts, is driven less by competition than by the strategic decisions of global players. Dedicated, systematic elimination of contingency has taken the place of risk as the vital force underlying capital accumulation and expansion.[5]

From this perspective we can see that the function of the ratings is to produce a dynamic hierarchy of corporations capable of producing known loss. At the summit are the pure global players which determine uncertainty for their sector, and at the lower end of the hierarchy are the successful medium and small companies operating in

---

[5] Analysts' conviction that the larger the unit, the easier it is to control loss and generate growth, places enormous pressure on corporations to expand through merger and acquisition rather than internal growth. For a statistical analysis of the growth in the number of global players since the 1970s, see Navaretti and Venables (2004). These authors unambiguously interpret the drive towards larger units as progressive in relation to the underlying viability of capitalism. For a critique of this same trend, see Ho (2009).

a single country or region whose activities have little if any impact on global trends – what one analyst I spoke to referred to as 'pond life'.

The progressive dynamic is, therefore, no longer envisaged – if it ever was – as driven by the transactions between a multitude of competing units. Economic progress is neither an innate tendency nor the chance result of millions of strategic decisions. It is, according to this view, the product of rational strategic choices of corporations in general and of major players in particular.

Jane affirmed this when she described how knowledge of executives' strategic choices is now the most important criterion for the prediction of future loss. The new dependence of corporations on the ratings has given analysts unprecedented access to long-term strategic plans. As Jane was at pains to explain, the criteria have not changed. Since the 1930s they have remained the same. There is no question of introducing anything new: 'But there has', she stressed, 'been a change in *emphasis*'.

The material basis for the guarantee was beginning to come into focus. The idea that the quality and the quantity of the data are sufficient to explain analysts' confidence in the guarantee is misleading as long as we assume that analysts derive their analysis from the competitive model of capitalist economy. Under the competitive model, raising capital on prediction would *presuppose* high levels of uncertainty, where the assumption is that causes of loss are limitless and the prediction, however well supported by the evidence, is a hypothesis, an estimate of the chances of something happening. Under the competitive model, uncertainty is a result of the spontaneous actions of many thousands of economic entities operating under competition. Hence, investment was traditionally made under the assumption of risk – the possibility of loss or gain.

The basis of analysts' confidence in the guarantee is indeed the data but this means something quite different once we know that the most significant data are derived from the strategic priorities of a relatively small group of major players whose activities are believed to determine patterns of future loss. Accepting a rationalist model, where, under conditions defined by analysts, measurable uncertainty results from the right strategic choices, the burden of guarantee falls on corporate executives. What analysts are actually guaranteeing shareholders is that executives in charge of investment grade corporations will adopt strategies that generate low uncertainty. The guarantee rests on a consequentialist assumption about the effectiveness of executives' intentions. However, the data derived from executives' intentions ultimately draw their power from the prior assumption that the right strategic choices can radically reduce or even eliminate unexpected loss.

Analysts' dependency on the rationalist model of the economy, which favours companies that are capable – according to their calculations – of generating low uncertainty, corresponds with the change in shareholders' attitude towards risk and the dramatic shift felt at corporate level, from corporations' dependency on shareholders' willingness to risk loss, to shareholders' dependency on corporate executives' capacity to avoid uncertainty.

From an anthropological perspective, the point of interest is the change in value which is introduced by investors' dependence on a rationalist model and the switch to investment criteria that no longer take share-holders' willingness to trade uncertainty for return to be an objectively necessary feature of capitalist economy. Through its dependence on a rationalist evaluative framework, the international investment community has effectively changed what it regards as essential to the future viability of capitalism. Driving uncertainty out of the system in an effort to create a safe invest-ment environment where levels of risk can be controlled is the essential dynamic. By virtue of investors' con-viction that control of market share guarantees the measurable uncertainty they are seeking, this dynamic serves to favour consolidation over and above market competition.[6]

Although credit rating analysts are themselves agents of this transformation, there is, so far, no evidence that they (or indeed the international investment commu-nity) acknowledge the process of transformation itself. On the contrary, the positive value attached to the new relation between low uncertainty and profit is treated as if it were consistent with the competitive ideal.

Leaving aside for the moment whether analysts' assumption of continuity with the past is a conscious rhetorical device, it is worth taking a moment to

---

[6] The classical model of market economy recognizes an inbuilt tendency towards monopoly, which has its source within the firm and the desire of those in charge to dominate market share in order to influence prices and control the quantity traded. In classical theory, the state – a force external to the market – is required to impose sanctions to counter this tendency. Here, however, we have the reverse. The external force favouring consoli-dation over and above competition is embodied by three major credit rat-ing agencies (Fitch, Moody's and Standard & Poor's) officially approved by the United States Security and Exchange Commission and designated 'nationally recognised statistical rating organizations'.

examine the elements that, taken together, serve to mask the underlying shift in context. Analysts do not spontaneously draw attention to the contradiction between the values underpinning the assessment criteria and the competitive ideal. There is, however, a presupposition on the part of many of us listening to them that their evaluative criteria are compatible with market competition. The two independent tendencies, taken together, contrive to conceal the radical shift from a competitive to a rationalist model. So, for example, when a financial analyst is quoted as saying, 'We have assessed the risk', we are likely to take this to mean that the assessment was drawn from the results of millions of independent investment decisions. It would go without saying that analysts hold the success of the capitalist dynamic to reside in competition and that their ability to cost risk is the result of improvements in statistical and mathematical techniques that have permitted them to overcome the limitations that a market dynamic used to present. The association of 'risk' with loss or gain remains unaffected. It is *both* a product of market competition and susceptible to determinate probabilities. There is nothing to suggest that, for analysts, the term 'risk' denotes a phenomenon that can be accurately measured and controlled to the extent that the underlying material uncertainty has been eliminated. There is nothing to suggest that for them the once-vital association between potential loss and profit has been broken.

The context in which we understand analysts' activity is, by and large, defined by the prior assumption that they are working under the hypothesis of competition which grounds our understanding of how assessments are achieved. In this scenario, the misplaced assumption that advances in mathematical and statistical methods combined with advances in technology have overcome the measurement problems once posed by market competition serves to mask a radical underlying change in context.

The same issue also arises with the term 'prediction'. Without a clear understanding of the foundational premises from which analysts draw the data, it would be difficult to perceive that, for analysts, 'prediction' is not primarily an expression of a statistical probability but an expression of the density of strategies geared to eliminating contingency from the system.

Hence, our own presupposition that credit analysts make their calculations on the basis of the competitive model serves to ground the assumption of a fundamental continuity between pre-finance and finance capital, and conceals the all-important shift from a conception of the economy that takes loss as a condition of gain to one where loss is seen as a threat to profit. This fundamental change in values is nowhere more clearly expressed than in analysts' use of the term 'entrepreneur'.

Analysts would often comment that investors will not go along with a gamble. I asked John whether this meant the end of the entrepreneurial company.

> John: If there is adequate cash flow to cover the risk then the rating won't be changed. Corporation X has a new project in Canada requiring enormous capital investment. I have not changed the rating because of the risk.

In other words, if future loss is known and there is evidence of adequate liquidity to cover that loss, then he will not penalize the company. From within the context of the competitive model, this is the same as saying that

what the press have to say about the way we handled Enron.

Me: It was investment grade. The criteria did fail.

Jane: Yes of course. But what everyone forgets is that before it collapsed it was rated triple B+. If we had downgraded, it would have collapsed and we would have been blamed for precipitating bankruptcy.

Me: But isn't the point, rather, that it was rated investment grade. And surely the real question is how do you know whether other quality companies are not just as vulnerable as Enron?

Jane: Fraud has terrible consequences but fraud on this scale is rare. Everything depends on people revealing their risk exposure truthfully. Everything depends on the auditors' knowing how to tell.

Me: I cannot see how you would be able to uncover a *collective* attempt to deceive you. Enron's actual debt to capital ratio was 80 per cent contrasted with the 57 per cent ratio reported by them.

Jane: Auditors are ten times more vigilant after Enron. Auditors have tightened up. They've improved disclosure on off balance sheet investment and they're writing about companies that refuse to give the disclosure. Analysts [for their part] are now asking better questions, they are reading the fine print. We are training their ears to get a little more attentive.

Me: But if there is a concerted attempt among the executive and internal auditors to mask vulnerabilities, it's hard to imagine the kinds of questions that would reveal that.

Jane: The ability to judge risk is the ability to judge the funding structure. [Pause] We rely on audited statements. [Pause] We are hamstrung by audited statements. If lying accountants sign off on a fiction. . .

She didn't finish the sentence. She'd made her point, the atmosphere was tense and I changed the subject.

What preserves the system and the validity of the methodology is the statistical rarity of severe external threat, of which fraud is an instance. The rationalist model and the method from which it is drawn are seen as highly stable. Under normal conditions, risk will continue to be measurable. For credit analysts, the problem is the unfair reputational damage that the unexpected crisis causes. On a separate occasion, Jane explained how frustrated they were by the difficulties brought about by Enron and how hard the agency had to work to avert the damage, which, she said, was understandable though quite unfair.

Fraud on this scale, then, is categorized as a violent and rare external event – such as might be imposed on a company by the collapse of a currency in which it is heavily invested. It shocks, but does not fundamentally threaten, the system. The collapse of Enron did not destabilize the economy. The knock-on effects were disruptive, disastrous for those people and businesses immediately affected, but did not threaten the fundamentals. The economy absorbed the shock and the domain of predictable loss still sets the boundary for the guarantee.

The same arguments have been advanced to defend the ratings in face of the more recent bank failures. No one was in a position to know the size and global reach of the subprime mortgage market. No one, including credit analysts, held these data in aggregate. The subprime crisis which led to the bank failures counts, therefore, as a violent and rare *external* event, which has led to 'bad times'. There is no question that faith in the probabilities is still justified. The implication of this mode of reasoning is that nothing, not even the collapse of capitalism itself, will raise suspicion about the method and the status of its underlying axioms. Crises per se and the failure to predict them not only do not invalidate the method, they do not even open it to scrutiny.

Knowing they cannot predict a crisis is not an excuse for complacency. Analysts work hard to identify the causes of failed predictions. Sometimes, it is a question of implementing the right processes to correct for the problem. As Pierre in the London office said, 'The historical data show we have been taking into account all the necessary factors: over 15 years, triple A-rated companies show only 5 per cent default. Triple C shows 70 per cent default. The fact that each category shows a slightly higher default rate is proof that we are doing it right.'

There is no reason for analysts to assume that, once this particular crisis has been resolved, the world economy will not resume previous rates of growth, something for which they like to take some credit.

The image of the economy that emerges from analysts' wish to focus on method creates the illusion of harmony between analysts' dependency on strategic priorities that avoid unexpected loss and the intentions of corporate executives. From analysts' description of their method, it would appear that their primary concern is indeed with calculation and that the incentive of a high rating is all that is necessary to create a domain in which risk can be calculated.

3
Entitlement

During the many conversations about method not once did analysts spontaneously mention any meetings with executives. I knew that interviews were an important part of the assessment process, but this was not something they alluded to, and as the weeks passed it became increasingly difficult to hang on to the idea of routine contact between the two camps, let alone of a profound and extensive conflict.

In retrospect, this eclipsing of the conflict seems extraordinary. But the collective force of the fiction of a separation between the two worlds whose only tangible connection is the material flow of data – an effortless movement from the corporations to the rating agencies and on to shareholders – permitted the idea of an opposition just to slip away to the point where I felt I must have seriously overestimated it.

I had to return to my original field notes to understand why it was that the conflict had initially appeared so powerful and unquestionable. Reading just a few pages of description brought its magnitude back into the foreground and I returned to the credit rating agencies with one question: why do you meet with executives?

Here are the immediate responses from six analysts in order of seniority.[1]

John (director, New York):

> Direct exposure means we get some impression as to how they articulate their strategies, what their backup plans are, how knowledgeable they are about their competitors, etc. We can assess their credibility, their competence. We look at whether they have the skill to pull it off . . . This is linked to credibility. *Did they stick to the plan or did they do something else?* If a company gets stretched then only companies with credibility will be given the benefit of the doubt, *if* they have a plan to solve their problem. [His emphasis.]

Phil (director, New York):

> I call it a negotiation skill. When I go into companies I am negotiating for data. I have to use cajoling language, smarts. I have to ask the right questions and if they don't want to answer it I have to find another way to ask the same question.

There was a long pause during which I said nothing. Then Phil added:

> I would call it negotiation. I would definitely call it negotiation. Although in Guantanamo they probably call it negotiating as well.

---

[1] The analysts quoted rate companies globally. None of the analysts quoted were in charge of rating corporations in which I had carried out fieldwork. The point here is the structural nature of the conflict. Each side knows the other as incapable of meeting the needs of capital.

Phil is the director who, at the beginning of my field-work in the credit rating agencies, wanted to deflect attention away from the idea that analysts are directing executives' decision-making.

David (senior analyst, New York):

> Companies have to respond to the double digit growth objective. This has to be translated down to each unit. We try to get an appreciation of what their potential is. We go into levels of detail as we think appropriate. The devil is in the details. We want them to make a broad commitment to being a certain kind of credit rating. If a company has a commitment to being a triple B, they cannot make risky acquisitions. There are capital constraints that trickle down . . .
>
> Companies come to us for help and advice. This does not mean that all companies have to proceed in the same way. They can do it stupidly or intelligently. But investors have become highly unforgiving. Twenty years ago as a CEO I could do a pretty pathetic job and I didn't have to worry about job security. But now I'm concerned – that's human nature. One individual can scare off investors and create havoc for a company. The potential for a liquidity crisis is much greater than it used to be. It translates into risk for the CEO. It all points in one direction.

Pierre (analyst, London):

> [We meet with executives] to check for inaccuracies. The numbers are important, but we want to get to know the management, we want to get to know the strategy. Accounting information is important, but strategy is even more important.

Jan (analyst, Paris):

> That's how you keep in touch with the business, ultimately

everything comes from the business. Our work is not just about numbers, it is about judgement.

Otto (junior analyst; Frankfurt):

[We meet with executives in order] to reconcile discrepancies in the data. We have to drill down to find the reason. For example, I might notice a weak clause in a contract with a supplier. I would want to know if they had it in all their contracts, I would want to see if it was multiple. They might not want to admit the error. The meeting could get tough. I would say I don't accept what you say. This is when you start to smell the sweat. The truth is the more open they are, the more likely it is they will get what they want. They don't seem to understand. If a person doesn't answer the question you have to find the reason. That's why face to face meetings are important.

Analysts' general disillusionment with executives' ability to manage increasingly pervaded each discussion.

They're careless, they're not careful.

There is a natural tendency for people to be reckless with other people's money, to take unnecessary risks.

They don't realize that the money does not belong to them, it belongs either to the banks or to the shareholders.

They don't know how to focus.

They don't pay attention to the figures.

If you listen to *them* there *are* no risks.

James [head of a US listed triple B-rated company] is a Rhodes Scholar, [but] his presentation was live with inaccuracies. How do you motivate these people to get it right?

There was nothing ambiguous about their engagement with the corporate world, nothing hidden about the enormous pressure they have to exert on executives to ensure sound strategy.

Phil again:

> There is an *inbuilt* temptation among CEOs to play for high stakes – after all, it is not *their* money. To make exciting, reckless decisions with other people's money is tempting. I have a confrontational style. Recently a CEO saw red. He was a marine. I thought he was going to jump over the table and strangle me. He swore he was not going to make this acquisition. I said, but you said that last time, why should I believe you? Some of these executives just have an empire mentality.

Pierre:

> There have been episodes where they [CEOs] get abusive. It depends to some extent on the personality of whoever is talking to them. I tell my analysts to say 'I'm not going to continue the conversation if you can't conduct yourself properly'. They can threaten to go to the papers about how stupid we are or threaten to go over our heads to speak to our CEO. But we feel we are independent and professional.

Julie:

> There is no better way to keep management on its toes than for management to know if they don't achieve earnings growth they'll be dismissed. Shareholders are saying you have to show x per cent increase – if you don't, I'm going to replace you. They don't like it but it's a change forcing corporate growth.

Jeff:

> We always encourage analysts to focus on strategy, it has always been factor 'x'. But can management execute it?

The tension will always be there. Of course management don't like to be questioned and to justify their results. They say, judge us in three years. *But if we just let them off the hook*, where's the challenge, where's the achievement? [His emphasis.]

And Jacques:

Shareholders just don't trust them.

There is no question of analysts' right to approve executives' strategic priorities and to ensure they are being properly implemented according to standards set down by the rating agency. It does not, however, occur to analysts that the recklessness, the desire to withhold data, and a 'inability to focus' may largely follow from their own flawed expectations.

Be that as it may, what analysts see as an 'inbuilt' tendency towards irresponsibility gives them no choice but to fight – really fight – to ensure executives act on agreed objectives. It was striking that not a single example of a competent, reliable executive was spontaneously mentioned. They do exist. When I pushed analysts on this point they would mention names. But the extravagance of the language – 'empire mentality', 'inability to pay attention' – and the generic terms in which they criticize executives strongly imply that driving uncertainty out of the system is seen by analysts as a battle against a particular pathology that has to be controlled by means of threat and intimidation.

The seamless shift from an emphasis on numbers to acknowledgement of conflict was truly extraordinary and raises a question as to why analysts did not initially want to speak about it. One reason for their reticence would be a desire to maintain investor trust.

In this world of statistics, investors need no reminding that, regardless of the sophistication of the modelling techniques, if the primary data are inaccurate, the probabilities are in effect unknown. There would therefore be little incentive to draw public attention to the additional uncertainty introduced by the difficulties executives have in keeping to agreed strategies.

In as far as there is a conscious ideological motive here, the aim would be to prevent shareholders from becoming aware of the problems they encounter in securing the data they need.

Phil's initial reluctance (described in chapter 2) to discuss the direct power analysts feel they are forced to wield over the corporations was not necessarily motivated by a wish to cover up their attempts to impose new investment criteria. It now seems much more probable that Phil wanted to draw my attention away from the issue of the reliability of the primary data. Thus, a conscious intention to cover up the conflict – if that is what it is – does not necessarily entail an awareness that they are doing anything other than enforcing established investment criteria. From the analysts' perspective, the battle is not between two theories of productive capital but between rational and irrational approaches to investment practice.

But this explanation does not help us to understand the openness with which they responded to my direct question about the reason for these meetings. The problem with the idea that their initial reluctance stemmed from a straightforward desire to mislead is that analysts – including Phil – discussed the conflict with me in full knowledge that I would be publishing this material.

Certainly no one acted as though they were aware of the shift from a presumption of harmony to one of suspicion and conflict. It may be that they have little, if any, experience of someone from outside the agency spending time with them, and their openness in this case could be a result of my apparent transition from an outsider to someone occupying a more ambiguous position – a transition which perhaps they themselves did not perceive.[2]

In this new context, far from trying to hedge, analysts were keen to enter into discussion, often lasting two to three hours, and many times I was invited to return should I want to discuss the matter further. My impression each time was that they felt I had finally arrived at what was really important. My sense of it was that they wanted me to know how hard they have to work to ensure capital is directed towards earnings growth and how dedicated they are to the task.

It does not necessarily follow, then, that a desire to conceal the conflict implies that analysts are acting irresponsibly towards investors who rely on the competence of their calculations. They are, after all, insisting on the correct application of sound principles. They take responsibility for the result and do everything in their power to make certain the threat to the economy presented by incompetence is held in check. Vigilance and intimidation work and from this standpoint, to the extent that analysts are covering up anything, it would

---

[2] Analysts' lack of recognition of the impact on me of the discrepancy between the ideal of harmony and the reality of conflict does not necessarily imply the two versions appear incompatible to them. I did not want to push them on this issue, however, because I was concerned not to deflect attention from the more important question of the conflict itself.

be the fact that what they have to do to keep the economy on course is far *more* than people realize.

The extent to which analysts collectively and consciously protect the ideal of harmony is difficult to assess. What is demonstrable, however, is that there is an explicit contradiction between the ideal of a cooperative handling of investment capital and the reality of conflict, and that both versions are articulated aspects of analysts' experience.

What is really impressive is that both versions have the same unintentional impact: to mask the breach in continuity of the investment principle which analysts themselves are insisting on. Moreover, there is no evidence that analysts see themselves as doing anything other than enforcing established investment principles. The downward pressure they exert is in the service of continuity. From their perspective, the altercation is not with history but with irrational CEOs.

The subjective dimension of analysts' experience serves to obfuscate a historical break in continuity of the investment principle without entailing ideological intention. Analysts genuinely do not appear to grasp the possibility that executives, for their part, may not be acting recklessly and so resisting the objective requirements of capital, but opposing a model of the economy which mistakenly identifies unpredictability with loss. The degree of analysts' commitment to the idea that the criteria are neutral explains their sense of entitlement. Indeed, they appeared to be so sure of their position that it was impossible to imagine them grasping even the possibility that their understanding of what constitutes genuinely unpredictable loss, and their intolerance of any event that – according to their judgement

– is indicative of a lack of attention paid to risk, could appear to others as simple ignorance of the principles on which profit is made.

If the neutrality of the criteria is taken for granted, however, then opposition can only be a sign of incompetence or irresponsibility. The pressure analysts have to exert on executives to ensure sound strategy would not, in itself, lead them to question the neutrality of the criteria and their assumption that rational executives will recognize their validity. The interpretive framework does not depend for its coherence on the capacity of executives in general to adapt to the needs of capital; it depends, rather, on rational executives being so adapted. Here, the identification of the criteria with rationality is absolute. If we accept the neutrality of the criteria, this makes logical sense. But from a rational point of view, a general tendency among executives to resist the needs of capital surely calls for some explanation. One would imagine analysts would be highly engaged in trying to explain the fact that the very people on whom we all depend for continuity and growth are not behaving rationally much of the time; yet analysts seem to take the degree of incompetence in the system in their stride.

At first I found this perplexing. But the more I thought about it, the more I realized just how much authority lies behind the idea that there exists an inherent tendency among executives to act irresponsibly. The argument that, because executives do not own the companies they run, they have little incentive to act in the owners' interests has been a part of the economic canon since Adam Smith.[3] What modern economists

[3] See Smith (1976), p. 741.

call the 'agency problem' – the tendency of managers to be reckless with other people's money – is treated by many economists as a fundamental problem of capitalism. For them, the question is not *whether* this tendency exists but how to develop incentives to counter it.

Since the 1970s the 'agency problem' has formed part of an interpretation of recent economic history that is widely accepted by a body of influential academics for whom the idea carries a normative status.[4] The problem, however, is derived from a motivational theory that is taken as self-evident and rules out from the start the possibility that executives might identify, for example, with the creative process of *making* profit rather than with the goal of profit as an end in itself. Nor does the a-priori status given to irresponsibility allow for the possibility that integrity may count in executives' emotional make-up.

Phil's historical account of the rise of the rating agencies, I realized in retrospect, corresponded with the prevailing hypothesis. As he explained, the increase in influence and power of the agencies coincided with the general loss of shareholder confidence in executives' capacity to manage responsibly. The self-evident quality of the idea that suddenly executives could not be trusted may well find its source in the authority of a theory which precedes their experience, which is then found to be consistent with 'observed behaviour'. This may be as true for shareholders as for credit analysts. In the case of analysts it cannot be ignored that an assumption of irresponsibility adds to the

---

[4] Jensen and Meckling (1976).

agencies' legitimacy, which more than ever is needed by shareholders.

The authority that lies behind the idea that conflict between owners and those in charge of the company is intrinsic to capitalism would make sense of an inherent tendency among executives towards irresponsibility. However, being predisposed towards a theory is not the same thing as unconditional acceptance. If pushed, how would analysts defend the idea that executives are predisposed towards recklessness. Do analysts, for example, ask why they themselves are not so inclined?

When I asked analysts directly how they accounted for executives' general unreliability, their reply was to the effect that, well, it's just human nature. This is another way of saying that there is a predisposition among people to behave irresponsibly – a non-explanation. The important ethnographic point, however, is that this answer appears to them to be unassailable. Moreover, the designation carries a strong moral component.

When Jacques told me, for example, 'They just don't want to take responsibility for the outcome' and then added, perhaps for my benefit, 'well that's human nature', it came across as a not terribly effective attempt to smooth over what had become, if it wasn't always, a highly judgemental attitude. Pierre was invoking human nature to demonstrate his understanding of executives' difficulties but he was, at the same time, holding executives to a strict standard of personal liability. Here, the term 'human nature' is moralistic and denotes human weakness which manifests itself as irresponsibility and/or incompetence which can, and should, be overcome independently by each person.

The generic failure of executives to pay attention to risk is explained in terms of failure of will. Failure of will then becomes a powerful default explanation for the occurrence of unpredictable loss.

Locating the capacity to overcome uncertainty within each person's will justifies analysts' single-minded and uncompromising attitude in relation to executives, which, in the domain of conflict, acts as a provocation. When significant unexpected loss occurs, analysts are predisposed to assume that executives have acted irresponsibly. This attitude sets the scene for conflict, well illustrated in the quotes above.[5]

But this takes us no nearer to understanding why analysts do not seem to be aware of the inconsistency in executives being victims of their 'nature' while analysts are not. The explanation can be found in a widely held principle of the uniformity of human nature and in accepted premises about the nature of science and, in particular, mathematics.[6]

As we have seen, neutrality is integral to analysts' claim to objectivity. Analysts interpret executive hostility in light of their commitment to each company's equality before rational criteria so that hostility is indicative of

[5] When I asked analysts directly if they would accept adverse circumstances as a legitimate explanation for unexpected loss, they said, 'Of course!' In chapter 2, I described how the first objective of the assessment process is to establish whether a company is operating in an environment where loss can be accurately predicted. But this does not affect analysts' view that executives in general act irresponsibly, thus placing analysts in the position of having to enforce the criteria.

[6] In writing this and the following two paragraphs, I benefited from ideas put forward in the Introduction to Toren (1999).

failure to overcome nature through the use of reason. This attitude corresponds with a prevailing concept of science. According to this view, science is possible only to the extent that human reason can be wrested from the messier aspects of human nature. Scientific rationality is, ideally, reason uncontaminated by desire and other human passions and, at least since Pythagoras (if not before), reason finds its most perfect expression in mathematical form. Credit analysts may well imagine they have the advantage over executives in this respect: their facility with numbers and the fact that they excel at highly abstract calculation serve to sustain their idea of themselves as having overcome human weakness in this sense, at least in respect of their professional ideal.

The human nature explanation is fundamental to an interpretive framework which, by virtue of the familiar association of reason and the capacity for abstraction, makes the distinction between reasonable analysts and unreasonable executives appear natural.

The assumption of inherent irresponsibility among executives operates within a much wider frame of reference that finds its authority in pre-established principles which serve to create the illusion of an incontestable reality. Paradoxically, opposition to the criteria, far from prompting analysts to question its presuppositions, serves to affirm executives inherent predisposition towards irrationality. This leaves analysts free to concentrate on enforcing the right principles without the burden of having to ask themselves if the principles on which they are insisting are the only viable ones.

At one point I pushed a director:

But you *must* be aware that executives can have reason to criticize the criteria?'

His answer was uncompromising:

What executives think has nothing to do with it. The assessments are neutral.

But the assumption that rational people will see the obvious – namely, that the investment criteria are neutral – is illusory. People occupying different positions in the economic structure think very differently and, contrary to what analysts imagine, the idea that there exists a single set of universal criteria corresponding to a single set of values is false and purely a feature of their subjectivity. Because for them it is the sensible economic activity of rational individuals that is the basis for cohesion of the capitalist economy, it cannot occur that this rational individual may himself be in the service of a particular *definition* of productive capital, born of a moral economy that has arisen independently of the economy over which the analysts believe they now reign.

The rationalist model that insists on a single, universal set of investment criteria is highly resilient. In so far as it organizes analysts' experience and determines their perceptions, it places them outside history with respect to consciousness but at the centre of a powerful transformation with respect to their own activities. From an ethnographic point of view, we can now legitimately speak of history as a force external to consciousness. In as far as the rationalist model encompasses analysts' experiences, the break with history is, for them, quite literally, unimaginable. They cannot see the meaning and the value of their actions – *how* these actions are incorporated into the overarching dynamic of the relations that define the present situation.[7]

In the next chapter I look more closely at the relation between consciousness and history, at the capacity of these particular analysts to step outside the rationalist model. Here I want to point out that there is an analytical distinction to be made between a given interpretive framework that assimilates experience and organizes perception and the relation between this framework and the external reality within which it is operating. Analysts often come up against realities that are not provided for by the rationalist model. These bits of reality that don't quite fit are seen as paradoxes for which they can find no solution. The conclusion that we might have otherwise drawn – that faith in their ideal of science and human nature stems from a temperamental predisposition to deal only in certitudes – is challenged by the fact that analysts face up to the paradoxes they encounter, refusing to ignore or to rationalize contradictory experience. Indeed, analysts' inability to explain the paradoxes is evidence for the astonishing resilience of the rationalist framework which holds up against intellectual integrity and a capacity to tolerate doubt.

[7] The analytical focus on the rationalist moral economy is not meant to imply that it is any more or less rational than the contingent moral economy. My working assumption is that an interpretive framework of any degree of sophistication is likely to contain serious flaws and contradictions. In contrast to the contingent moral economy which has been dissected and analysed for over 200 years, the rationalist model is only just beginning to come to the fore.

4
Doubt

From within the rationalist moral economy, the conflict between credit analysts and executives does not provide analysts with any suggestion of a disjuncture between their views and external reality. Indeed, the rationalist framework is so successful in assimilating the conflict that it begins to look as if points of incompatibility not only do not occur, but cannot occur in principle. But this is not so. Tensions do exist between the analysts' experience with executives and preconceived notions. But from within the rationalist framework, these tensions can only appear as irresolvable paradoxes for which analysts find no solution. On the one hand, they are unable to resolve them. On the other, a fundamental intellectual integrity prevents them from making easy rationalizations, which they are perfectly capable of doing. The two examples given below lend insight into the hold the rationalist model has on analysts' imagination in the face of evidence that directly questions the universality of the rationalist principle.

Analysts are well aware that even those CEOs and

FEOs for whom they have the highest regard, and whom they categorize as rational, work hard to present their companies in the best possible light. However:
Nick (senior analyst):

> To my mind they [executives] take it too far. They go through rehearsal sessions . . . [He raises his hand to his head in exasperation.] I can't believe it. . . .. You've been a CEO for ten years. Why do they have to rehearse? Is it that they're not knowledgeable? There's this mythology that has grown up around it [the rating]. Merrill Lynch sits with them, prepares them, holds their hand. I don't understand it. I just don't understand it. If you know the business, you know. If you know the business, all you need to do is to sit down and talk about it in a reasonable way. [He shakes his head.] I don't understand why they chafe under it.

And later,

> I would love to know what they tell them. You should go to Goldman Sachs, Merrill Lynch, talk to them, find out what they do.

He wrote down the name of the department and the name of the man I should telephone.

As Nick said, if executives know their business, all they need to do is to sit down and talk about it. So why can't they just talk about what they know?

Nick was referring here to executives whom the analysts trust, executives whom they know are willing and able to meet the objective requirements of capital. Responsible, confident and successful executives are the one category that should not present any problem. Yet these same executives, who know that the data they produce can only affirm their competence – their success is, after all, a consequence of having met the requirements of the criteria – go to enormous trouble and expense to seek reassurance. It makes little sense to analysts that, knowing their success is a consequence of having kept to the criteria, executives would *chafe* under them.

If Nick were thinking purely practically, there would be no issue. These executives can be relied on to deliver. The reason their behaviour rankles, the reason it cannot be put down to a general insecurity, is because the identification of competence with voluntary acceptance of the criteria has to be true if the rationalist model is to remain coherent. Whether analysts see it consciously in these terms is difficult to say but it was impressive that Nick found executives' inability just to 'say what they know' problematic. The internal institutional dialogue had not provided him with an answer.

Well into the second hour of our second meeting, David raised an issue which he and his colleagues had been concerned with for some time. For years, he said, they had been working with Roland, the chief executive of a major player with a consistently high rating. Roland personified the ideal CEO, reliable and trustworthy. 'Someone like Roland', David said, 'you meet twice a year just to check how things are going'.

Then he continued:

We thought we had a great relationship. We thought we knew him. Then we read an interview with him in [one of the top US business magazines]. They did a profile on him. They asked him what was the best thing that ever happened to him in his life. And he said something like, the birth of my daughter or meeting my wife, and then they asked him what was the worst thing that ever happened and he said, meetings with the credit analysts. We were all distressed about it. It is not our objective to have him feel it is a bad experience. We telephoned him immediately. We took him out to lunch, to build bridges, to a *very* good restaurant. I hope we got the message across.

Later David insisted I find the magazine:

Read the article. Look it up. It was August 2000 and something. I've forgotten the exact date.

After more than four years David and his colleagues (he uses the first person plural) continued to be disquieted by this event. Their concern was not with Roland's resentment and anger at having to work with credit analysts, but with their own lack of understanding about the *source* of his anger and unease about what *their* lack of understanding might represent. The revelation that meetings with you are the *worst* thing that ever happened in someone's life is quite something when it comes from someone you thought shared your interests.

Each of these narratives casts doubt on the unifying principle that rational (successful) executives embrace the investment criteria which ensure continuity of established and proven investment principles. Resentment and hostility towards the criteria are symptoms of executive failure and reveal an unwillingness to place the concerns of the company over and above their own narrow ambitions. The problem is that executives for whom analysts have so much regard do not necessarily accommodate the foundational assumption. Their hostility cannot be interpreted in terms of a failure of will.

The important point here is that analysts find this a problem. The fact that they want to understand it and to solve it – and cannot – is indicative of their intellectual integrity, the depth of their perplexity, and the resilience of their ideal of an inherent unity of interests between rational executives and rational analysts.

For reasons we can now begin to see, these analysts are barred from directing their attention to the foundational premises of their mode of thinking. This raises the possibility that their ideal of rationality cannot touch upon the possibility that it is not universally held. The paradox of the executives who meet the criteria and at the same time oppose it can only be resolved by positing the existence of another equally viable concept of rationality, which is inconceivable from within their interpretive framework.

The implication of an unshakeable *faith* in the neutrality of the criteria and the universality of the rationalist principle is that analysts are unable to perceive how the rationalist moral economy works or even that it exists as an identifiable entity.

The degree of analysts' commitment to this particular concept of rationality and all that it encompasses is not the result of a lack of a general capacity to doubt – if this were so, they would not be so vexed by the problem of competent yet hostile executives. Rather, both their commitment and their puzzlement in the face of executives' paradoxical hostility reflect the resilience of the rationalist interpretive framework, which on the one hand permits doubt, but, on the other, assimilates experience in such a way as to prevent the possibility of a viable alternative from arising.

Here we see how the nature of the commitment to the rationalist framework does not merely predispose analysts to certain choices of interpretation but demarcates what is imaginable. In as far as these particular analysts are unable to step outside this framework of reasoning, they can imagine capital being directed or *misdirected* according to a single universal principle. They cannot imagine that capital may be directed according to an alternative set of principles that would easily explain what they take to be paradoxical. They cannot imagine that a simple switch in value could make a risky world *a condition* of productive capital. Under the contingent model, unexpected loss, far from being a symptom of executive failure, is proof of their capacity to generate profit.

The rationalist model places the contingent moral economy beyond analysts' horizon of understanding. The ultimate paradox is that analysts' commitment to a single, universal rationality blinds them to the consequences of their own activities. The misconception that they are merely enforcing universally accepted and established investment principles masks the spectacular way in which they exert pressure on the direction of capital flow. From their perspective, however, they are doing no more than imposing what everyone knows is the only rational approach to investment.

What they imagine 'everyone knows', as we now see, is a product of a specific view of the world that not everyone shares. And to the extent that analysts believe that their view constitutes the consensus among rational people, their actual historical role – to introduce and enforce entirely new investment criteria – remains independent of their will and of their rationality. Or we might say that history is operating independently of their will, but not independently of their activity. In as

far as this is true, analysts do not understand the nature
of their agency.

But perhaps this conclusion is a little extreme. Perhaps
there's a more straightforward, pragmatic explanation. Could analysts simply be too busy to reflect on
and analyse the implications of their own presuppositions? Their inability to solve the paradox they find in
executives' attitudes may, on balance, reflect an external
constraint rather than their degree of faith in a particular concept of capitalist economy. If this were the case,
if time were the issue, the possibility that analysts could
become aware of the nature of their agency would exist.
The answer to this difficult empirical question hangs
on the extent of their commitment to their rationalist
model and whether *in principle* it prevents them from
imagining an alternative. I return this question in chapter 6.

The level of uncertainty analysts take to be inherent
in the economy is held to position executives in relation
to events in such a way that it is reasonable to assume
that given the right conditions, the correct strategy can
determine the course of events. Analysts' assumption of
a universal rationality is also a metaphysical assumption about the fundamental stability of the world. With
the exception of sudden and violent events, the future
is visualized as resembling the past in predictable ways.
Enron, the Asian currency crisis, and the collapse of the
banking sector are examples of external and unpredictable events. Under this rationalist model, the 'pragmatic
approach' will therefore consist in deducing future
scenarios on the basis of past experience. To hold this
pragmatism reasonably, one has to assume a low range
of inherent uncertainty in the environment.

The fiction of a consensus of continuity of investment criteria and of history derives from a metaphysical assumption about the stability in the world, and this metaphysical assumption makes it possible to agree, in objective terms, what constitutes a reasonable decision. In as far as analysts are committed to the idea that this degree of stability is a natural, immutable feature of the environment, and in as far as they have internalized it as *the* world through which people move, their capacity to perceive an alternative is going to be restricted.

If the idea of a single, universal rationality derives its appearance of naturalness from the foundational assumption of levels of uncertainty inherent in the environment, then when analysts enforce the criteria they are merely enforcing principles that belong to the natural constitution of the economy. In as far as assumed levels of uncertainty are taken to be inherent in the economic environment, the possibility of an alternative and viable way of perceiving the environment will lie outside the realm of nature.

In order to find the solution to the paradox posed by the hostility of competent executives to the criteria, analysts would have to be able to imagine an alternative to their metaphysical assumption. This would entail recognition that their concept of productive capital is a feature of their subjectivity.

The problem of consciousness – of whether analysts could, in principle, correct their misperception – is still outstanding. But, were they able rationally to re-examine their principles and methods, their claim to neutrality would fall apart. As long as rational means universal, the break-up of one idea will entail the collapse of the other.

The widely held view of recent economic history that interprets economic changes since the 1970s as progressive sides with the analysts in not perceiving the structural break in the investment principle. The lack of a strong alternative to this view helps to sustain the illusion that there exists a consensus (which includes everyone in the corporate world) that the global economy continues to operate on the basis of a single and universally held concept of productive capital.

Given the present balance of power – the dependence of corporations on credit analysts for investment capital – it is not in the interests of those working inside the corporations to try to correct this misperception. The covert opposition that exists within corporations does not make itself felt in the public domain. There are two elements to this last point. First, the level of analysts' conviction that brooks no challenge forces corporate executives to manipulate data and make it appear as though they too operate in a world of intended consequences. Because companies manipulate data, they are deeply compromised, and the main preoccupation with regard to analysts, shareholders and the public has to be with secrecy. Second, the fact that they are compromised means they cannot risk beginning a dialogue with other corporations on this issue. To open a genuine dialogue, executives would have to begin by acknowledging that they cannot meet the requirements, which would be tantamount to admitting that they are intentionally misleading credit analysts – a dangerous disclosure. So although individual executives may well be aware that the same powerful contradictions must apply across the board, this knowledge, even if it is generally held, does not provide the basis for collective action which would otherwise be in their gift. Shorn of this constraint, corporations would have the power and the resources to refuse to continue the pretence that they are adjusting to the criteria, and, in face of such pressure, analysts' perceptions and their demands would become irrelevant.

As we shall see in the next chapter, the routine manipulation of data means that corporations have a powerful interest in deflecting attention away from the breakdown in consensus. This is a truly fantastic state of affairs, which raises an important historical question: how do such forces so ingeniously combine to cause a breakdown in consensus to which neither camp ascribes a positive value? The overturning of established investment criteria compatible with market principles does not appear to be the result of design, but neither can it possibly be the result of chance.

This causal question I leave to historians. Here I want to say only that economic transformations within capitalist economy tend to be understood either in terms of the results of the spontaneous actions of individuals where an underlying alignment with progress (the invisible hand) is tacitly assumed (Friedrich Hayek, Milton Friedman), or in terms of conscious design where certain people take certain decisions for certain ends and these decisions set the economic course (the credit analysts). Here we have an instance of a transformation, however, where 'progress' – which resides in the elimination of risk from the system – is designed, while its historical effect – the rupture with past principles of capital accumulation – is independent of intention. Hence, in the new dynamic, 'progress' is no longer naturally aligned either with spontaneous action or with conscious intention.

The question of whether the institutional 'adaptations' and the shift to a set of values that favours consolidation that have been achieved constitute progress in relation to the underlying viability of capitalism has to be left to economists. What I can say, as an ethnographer and anthropologist, is that the myopia created by the analysts' rationalist model ensures for the present that analysts and investors are not brought to face the realities arrayed against them.

5
Contingency

High-tech industry, Europe

You have to understand, we're using techniques that have never been applied before. The fact is, most things that happen are things that you never, never believe would happen and all your calculations go out the window. Things happen that affect the whole picture, things that you would never consider looking twice at. But that's what I'm paid for, to solve the problem. My skill lies in solving problems.

At the end of a launch we reflect, learn what we can from our mistakes, draw out what we might be able to avoid next time. But, however successful the project, the day we go live everyone is down on their knees, praying 'please, please, please'. There is always the possibility of error. Things are never what they seem.

Tim is a team leader of a successful high-tech company operating in a classically entrepreneurial environment. He is responsible for digital systems installed in international trading rooms, including the World Trade Center in New York. The week following 9/11 we spoke by telephone. '*Four days*', Tim told me with pride. 'Four days and we were up and running.'

Even the wildest contingency can align itself with success.

Extractive industry, Central Asia

David is in charge of oil exploration. This was our third meeting and I was waiting for him to finish his telephone conversation. Well, perhaps not so much a conversation – he was out of control, shouting in a foreign language that I happen to understand: 'Fuck. Fucking son of a bitch. That fuck! That stupid fuck! That fucking son of a bitch!'[1]

He continued in this vein for a full minute before he stopped midstream and hung up. He said our trip to the drilling site had been cancelled. One of his men had had a road accident on a highway 200 miles south and they needed the helicopter to take him to hospital. He'd arrange our visit for another time. He invited me to what turned out to be a very alcoholic lunch where he was perfectly candid about the reasons for his outburst.

For over a year, in competition with virtually every other major oil company, he had been negotiating with the local government for the extension of exploration rights and he was on the verge of signing the deal when that morning he learned that the rights had gone to another oil company which had doubled the bribe and closed the deal. The person on the phone, he told me,

---

[1] Author's translation.

was his European boss. 'He knows me', David said; 'He knows when I need to let off steam.'

We are in a world where the unexpected hits often and hits hard. But there is a clear distinction between an unanticipated event that threatens a specific project and the uncertainty integral to expansion.

Pulp Mill, North America

I had travelled a day and a half to see the production manager. His secretary suggested I came back the next day, perhaps I'd have more luck then. He was involved in a tough union negotiation. The following day he did find a few minutes to meet with me. His first words were by way of apology.

> We need to introduce new machinery. We need to undercut a condition. How long do I go on talking about it? Two hours? Why not three? Why not five? What is enough? Do I want to take a strike? But a six-week strike or a two-week strike? The company is willing to take a strike. A two-week strike, but not a six-week strike. I've got two unions, one 80 per cent the size of the other and there is no centralized bargaining and no strong union leader.

He explained the background of the disagreement in some detail. And then:

> There's low unemployment, unions are strong and we're completely dependent on the price of labour. But this is all going to end. Contracting out keeps wages low, stops unionization.

Then he said sympathetically,

> They don't stand a chance.

The talk lasted about twenty minutes before he called Robert, one of his production supervisors, and asked him to give me a tour of the mill.

Robert began our tour by taking me to the top of the tower. Train cars filled with trees trailed into the forest as far as the eye could see. He then took me to the end of the production line where thousands of boxes of white paper were being forklifted onto trucks. 'How long do you think it takes to turn all those trees into paper?' he asked me with pride. I could not even make a guess.

Whether high-tech, extractive or manufacturing industry, uncertainty and its corresponding rationality manifests itself in managers' relation to the external world. To meet the goal of profit is to adapt judgement and resources to present circumstances. Swift recognition of a crisis, a cool head in the heat of the moment, and the capacity to apply past experience to a new situation are the qualities that make capital effective.

Managers openly discuss, and on occasion flaunt, the uncertainty they deal with every day. In a well-run company, the dividing line between a genuinely unavoidable loss and 'a management fuck-up' (to quote one manager) is seldom clear cut. Senior managers rely on experience to determine whether even multiple failures are a consequence of adverse circumstances or a genuine incapacity to manage. From within the context of a contingent economy, a manager's performance is assessed on the basis that circumstances beyond his control can, and often do, affect the result. The distinction between recklessness and external impact is not always obvious and certainly not measurable.

Indeed, failure to accomplish a given goal can be, and

often is, the result of management decisions – and here corporate executives would agree with the credit analysts – but, even then, it does not follow that a manager could reasonably have been expected to act otherwise. There can be no guarantee, however good the decision, that the outcome will align itself with the intention. The point is that an unpredictable environment is a result of the process of wealth creation itself. Even in a highly integrated corporation that has been categorized by analysts as a safe investment, the situation is always changing and a multitude of unanticipated events with potentially adverse effects face any manager striving to achieve even the narrowest goal. Hence enormous importance is attached to the capacity to react to the unexpected, which is at least as likely to be a deciding factor as good decision-making and luck. The unexpected event signals the *possibility* of loss, but without this possibility the potential for gain would not exist. Thus, unpredictability per se is not a threat to, but a condition of, productive capital.

It is on this issue of value and the tenacity with which analysts stick to the idea of risk as threat that the two worlds part. The a-priori identification of the unexpected event with a failure to 'control risk' has no place in a world where the unpredictable is a result of wealth creation.

As we have seen in chapter 1, prior to the 1980s, executives could rely on the fact that shareholders shared their ideals. For both, the virtue that lay in shareholders' willingness to risk their capital to the market was compatible with the immeasurable uncertainty deemed to be so vital to progress.

Given the disparity between the two perspectives, it is

easy to understand how unlikely it would be for anyone in a corporate environment to accept the legitimacy of the new constraints. No one is going to take seriously a motivational theory that aligns deviations from strategy with an irresponsible attitude. The problem is that this theory now underpins the decisions of credit rating agencies and other financial institutions that wield direct power over the corporation. The threat of such a principle entering into and adversely affecting the economic system is, as one CEO put it, 'the stuff of revolutions'.

Notwithstanding the threat to established and proven principles of capital accumulation and expansion, executives do not openly oppose the new criteria. Instead, they opt to engage in the pretence of accommodation while continuing to invest on the basis of what they hold to be sound principles. Hence, the protracted struggle between the two concepts of productive capital, between two worlds that continue to confront each other, remains silent.

The CEO quoted above spoke of revolution, but his reticence in face of what he sees as unstoppable pressures means that, like his counterparts in other companies, he too focuses on ensuring that his company is perceived by analysts to be operating in line with their expectations. However, behind a mask of consent, he continues to run the business on his own terms.

Building the fiction of a continuity of the investment principle has become an industry in itself, part of the infrastructure of the corporation. The version of a company's strategic priorities given to analysts – on the basis of which executives are interrogated – is only the beginning of the struggle to protect future viability by concealing immeasurable risk. Analysts' demands for proof that corporations are adapting strategy to their criteria means that to safeguard profitability, managers at all levels have to produce evidence that the new orthodoxy is being acted upon.

In what follows I compare how the contradiction between the rational and contingent concepts of productive capital plays itself out in the interstices of two corporations, and how in each case unique circumstances permit executives and their managers to 'reconcile' what they hold to be the objective requirements of capital with the new criteria in ways that leave little or no trace of a conflict in principle. One of the many paradoxes of the new status quo is that the fiction of consensus that executives and managers actively help to create reinforces the power and the authority of the ideals they so strongly oppose.

The first company – High Tech Digital Systems – operates in a competitive environment. Margins are tight and managers work under the pressure of knowing that a few major errors can quickly push the company into negative cash flow. The ratings downgrade that would inevitably follow would exacerbate the financial difficulties and put the existence of the company itself under threat. In the context of intense competitive pressure, the requirement to measure risk serves to threaten the domination of the contingent model within this company and the result is an amplification of immeasurable uncertainties in the working environment. The second example is a major player. It is an extraordinary irony that corporations whose strategies are believed by analysts to determine underlying patterns of loss, and on which the analysts rely so heavily for their data, are least constrained by the new orthodoxy. Aware of their market position, executives know that, while the threat of a drop in their rating could affect the cost of capital and/or temporarily affect share price, it would not threaten the existence of the company. A well-worked-out structural separation between the new demands and the principles on which the company is managed ensures that the requirement to identify risk exposure poses no threat to the domination of the contingent model within this company.

High Tech Digital Systems

High Tech Digital Systems (HTDS) is a highly successful company. Its status within the industry made it a catch for a multinational which bought HTDS in a bid to maintain its BB+ rating. The consolidated debt of the holding company was considerable and the acquisition was to be financed through additional borrowing. HTDS core activity is generated by 125 project teams who design and implement complex digital systems. Its prestigious client list includes the international trading rooms of banks and mutual funds, as well as the defence industry. The teams of highly qualified technicians are responsible, in other words, for developing and maintaining the digital systems that allow financial and other institutions to amass and analyse the vast amounts of statistical data that have transformed the global economy.

To maintain its investment grade rating, the holding company was expected to increase earnings growth while simultaneously sustaining a good cash-flow-to-debt ratio. To achieve this, they had to cut back on waste. The first act of the holding company, in relation to the subsidiary, was to cut its most expensive commodity – labour – and change the assessment of management's contribution to the company from measurement of time worked to measurement of output. The aim was to service the debt while simultaneously increasing earnings growth. To maintain the rating and lower the rate of interest, the holding company, in other words, was depending on fewer managers to produce the same quality product for less money.

Steve, a project manager, was the first to speak to me openly about the consequences of the labour cuts. Initially project managers were reluctant to discuss their views. However, once I convinced them that I understood that the new constraints had created a series of objective problems that they were not in a position to change, and having reassured them I was interested only in general principles and even their own personnel would not be able to trace what was said back to any individual manager, they began to discuss what they saw as the real effects of the cuts.

Steve told me how the two changes in labour policy, the labour cuts and the change in assessment criteria from measurement of time worked to measurement of output, meant that two team members now did the job of three. And where a line manager used to oversee two or three projects at a time, it was now likely to be four or five. The time and energy required to deliver a project are the same, so managers had to cut corners in every possible area to meet deadlines without reducing product quality. But this also meant a reduction in the time available for planning, so that everything was now done 'on the hoof'. But, Steve stressed:

We have to get it done and we have to get it right. If systems go down in an international trading room we lose 7 million dollars per minute.

Managers felt they had been doing well protecting existing margins but there was no question of an increase in earnings growth.

Explaining how the cuts had affected the quality of his life, Steve said that he now went weeks without seeing his children, and every holiday he was obliged to take his mobile phone and be on-call twenty-four hours a day. He repeated, '*twenty-four hours a day*'. This meant there was no time in the year when he could just be a father, a family man. He spoke to me at length about his alternatives, and he had clearly thought a great deal about how he might change his job and improve the quality of his working and family life. But, he said, there was no real alternative. Everywhere, things have changed radically. The deterioration in the quality of working life applied equally to other companies in this sector. He knew his competitors well and knew that moving firms was not a solution.

Against this background of a heavy increase in workload, new assessment processes had been introduced by the holding company, ratified by the board of the subsidiary, to assess risk. As described on page 13, note 1, legislation now requires directors to implement auditable processes to assess the company's risk exposure. Based on the rationalist model, these processes are designed to ensure that, as strategic priorities are translated into operational procedures, the risk to capital is understood. The board of the holding company appointed risk managers for each of its subsidiaries.

Their brief was to implement and supervise these proc-esses, and to report back to the board.

The risk assessment process consists of asking project managers to list the potential losses for each project and then to cost those losses. This was, on the surface, no more than a time-consuming exercise. But the problem, Steve explained, was that at least 50 per cent of losses incurred were genuinely unforeseeable. No matter how much time they had for planning, the high number of unexpected events that appeared in the field could not have been anticipated. To emphasize the ludicrousness of the expectation, John, a team leader, told me that 'from day one, costs can go anywhere'.

The inconsistency between expectation and reality was resolved by inventing 'known risks' which project managers then 'costed'. This inevitably left a wide margin between actual and listed causes of loss. While there was no moral conflict (they believed they had no alternative), it was demoralizing to be forced into a position where, to protect their projects and themselves from being judged against unworkable criteria, they had to take actions they felt to be wrong.

They were also acutely aware that their mis-statements were auditable. They were passed to the risk manager, who then made his report to the boards of the subsidi-ary and holding company, who in turn made it available to the auditors on request. In pretending to be able to meet the risk manager's objectives, project managers provided evidence of a strong material base for the effec-tiveness of the assessment procedure.

The ability to anticipate or identify the causes of future loss constituted the planning stage of the project which, prior to the cuts in labour, project managers had always done. But assessing risk under the assumption of extremely high levels of inherent uncertainty meant something quite different. Project teams would call in experts and spend a few days brainstorming to anticipate potential pitfalls. But it was understood that the exercise, however comprehensive, would not determine the course of events. The most important skill lay in being able to solve unpredictable problems as they arose. The misplaced assumption underlying the new risk assessment process, however, was that good planning could radically reduce or even eliminate unpredictable events.

Steve again:

> [Proper] risk assessment is an intellectual activity, it takes time to reflect. The fact is that we don't have the time. The more streamlined the company, the harder people have to work. The company can't provide the money and the people it would take to assess risk. The main pressure is to cut costs and increase profit margins. Lowering risk costs money they don't have. But demands on time and intelligence are increasing, while resources are either static or decreasing. We just have to deal with the consequences as they occur. It's all fire fighting.

For the time being, project managers can rely on their line managers, who side with them in opposition to the risk assessment procedures. But they are routinely misstating the cost of risk and it is not clear where the loyalty of senior management lies and whether, if found out, they will be held accountable.

When I asked project managers why they thought the processes were introduced, they attributed it to a loss of confidence in assessing performance on the part of the holding company's managers. Pressure from greedy shareholders and the demand to increase the revenue line had resulted in the introduction of an 'objective measurement' which was also supposed to improve efficiency. The effect, however, is counterproductive:

> The board thinks that risk assessments will make people work harder but it just leads to demoralization. It builds in a sense of failure and lowers productivity. My job is to protect my project managers. My job is to keep expectations reasonable. Making unreasonable demands on my project managers is bad for morale.
>
> (Graham, line manager)

The Workshop

Punctually at 8 a.m., twenty-four project managers were sitting at their desks listening to the risk manager's opening statements. He stood at the front of the room, chalk in hand. Attendance was compulsory.

Bill Deacon, the risk manager, opened with a half-hour lecture on the value of risk assessment as a management tool, stressing that his role was to help managers to improve their assessment techniques and increase their 'risk sensitivity'.

> If we were not good at managing risk, the company would not be successful. Risk assessment is a way of ironing out the unknowns ahead of time. It is business based on knowledge.

With this opening statement, Bill set the terms of reference for the workshop. The process he wanted to teach had five steps: identifying risk (brainstorming), prioritizing, calculating probability, choosing the appropriate mitigating strategy and, finally, costing the strategy.

Bill illustrated the process with case studies where managers had to read a project brief and then follow each of the five steps. Bill assessed each group's attempt. Success was measured by their ability to predict the course of events (as defined by Bill). Risk could be accurately measured only if unexpected events were anticipated. He gave his presentation with enormous confidence, reminding his audience that his brief was backed by the board of the holding company:

Don't forget, directors get paid according to how much revenue they deliver.

In a key exercise, Bill asked managers to provide real examples of causes of loss due to systems failure. By oversimplifying the conditions in which decisions were made – he did not once ask managers to describe the conditions – and emphasizing similarities between instances of loss rather than differences, the causes of loss were in each case made to appear self-evident. At no point were project managers called upon to describe what a risk looked like *at the time* of a decision. Bill did not allow for the possibility that the decision may have been the best decision, given the information at the time. Project managers, for their part, did not contradict him.

Perhaps the most astonishing aspect of the workshop was watching managers as they were drawn into the question of what they *should* have done to prevent a particular loss from occurring, colluding with the assumption – by no means demonstrated – that they could have acted otherwise. At all times, Bill's focus was on what he assumed to be managers' errors of judgement and what they must now do to improve their performance. Managers participated in the question-and-answer sessions, apparently accepting the validity of his criticisms. As a result, Bill was left free to believe that managers accepted that the principles he was propounding were reasonable, free to report back to the board that the workshops were a success, and that the guidelines for good corporate governance were being followed.

After the workshop, we did not even have time to get out of the door before a project manager whispered to me:

> Those who think that management is about advanced calculation don't know what management is.

Why did twenty-four project managers with a wealth of experience at their disposal sit in silence? Why did they choose not to mobilize their collective knowledge, preferring instead to carry out the pretence that they accepted the authority of the risk manager in relation to their own decision-making? Why did they not, at the very least, point out to him that the processes he wanted to see instated assumed a cost which projects could no longer bear?

As I have described above, for the time being project managers can rely on their line managers to protect them from being held accountable to the risk manager, or other senior managers who may identify with his cause. In this company, team leaders and line managers share the views of project managers and continue to make their assessments on the basis of traditional performance criteria.

But the appointment of the risk manager has introduced an ambiguity into the system. No one can be quite sure whether his performance criteria will at some point take over from that which project managers and others consider to be properly suited to the working environment. The holding company is, in effect, creating two hierarchies of authority with no formal relationship between them and managers do not know how this will evolve. Project managers are aware, for example, that the form-filling exercise is the first stage of a far more ambitious plan to identify cross-sections of risk. Bill was seeking board approval to assess the top ten forecasts from each project manager over a twelve-month period, which would entail comparing anticipated and actual causes of loss, and he seemed confident that he would get it. The momentum at the senior levels appeared to be worryingly in favour of the new orthodoxy, in which case project managers would be unlikely to want to express views that, from the perspective of the new ideals, could be interpreted as a reflection of their inability to assess risk. But they also knew that their silence would not solve the longer-term problem and that the likelihood of an increase in the risk manager's influence over the boards of the subsidiary and the holding company had created a new kind of uncertainty which might prove to be unmanageable.

Project managers are acutely aware of the contradiction between the centrality of their activity in the company – profit depends on their capacity to manage a wildly contingent environment – and the new pragmatism which has turned the anticipation of loss into a management principle. The general demoralization that has resulted is palpable, if not measurable.

Following the workshop, I asked Bill if he had

considered the possibility that managers may not, in fact, agree that his method of assessment is effective and if it may not be the case that they don't speak up because they know he has the backing of the board.

> Managers who feel threatened are managers who can't do it.

He went on to ask me if I knew of any techniques that would improve the company's selection procedure:

> We want to be able to assess who will be good at anticipating risk.

Bill Deacon, risk manager

If Bill had been aware of the contradiction between what he was demanding and the realities managers were facing – if managers had spoken up – his task would have been much more difficult. The fiction of consensus that made his task appear to him to be relatively straightforward depended partly on the continued silence of managers, but also on his own blindness to the realities that surrounded him.

In the car on the way back from another of his workshops, Bill told me that his move into risk management was followed by a nervous breakdown. His account of his illness gives us some insight into how irreconcilable demands in the environment can take the form of an internal psychological crisis. In Bill's case, the principle that loss can be anticipated and controlled was strongly tied to his identity. When he came up against external circumstances that could not be reconciled with this principle, his sense of self came under threat.

A number of things contributed, he said, including his wife's long illness. She had now recovered but it was the following event, he told me, that was the principal cause of the breakdown. He had accepted the post of risk manager, but, in order to have first-hand knowledge of what management faced, he had asked first to be put in charge of a project. His background training did not preclude this possibility.

In preparation he carried out a detailed risk analysis, bringing in expertise from every quarter to identify the risk exposure. But right away things began to go wrong and, within three months, he was $14 million over budget with the project far from completion. Within nine months he had managed to bring the loss back down to $6 million which, he told me, was unheard of – 'a miracle by any standards'. Then he became quite depressed when he realized that he was given no credit at all for pulling back so successfully and saving the company from a potentially much greater loss. Instead he was blamed for the $6 million he ultimately did lose for the company. This, he said, was a terrible experience and was the ultimate cause of his breakdown. The conclusion he drew from this experience was that his initial risk assessment had not been tight enough. 'We needed to tighten the assessment technique', he said.

A presentation to the board analysing his failure and showing what he had learned had secured him his current position.

Bill blamed himself for the whole fiasco and one can only respect him for taking full responsibility for the loss of revenue. What is truly astonishing, however, and tragic for him personally, is that it did not occur to him to ask whether some of the obstacles could *not* have been anticipated in objective terms, or even whether he could have responded more effectively to each crisis as it occurred. The rich and complex world that constitutes the resistant environment which project managers have to overcome to generate profit was, literally, beyond his imagination, and this was true in spite of his experience. His sense of self depended on the conviction that loss can be foreseen, and hence he was confined to explaining the causes of loss solely in terms of his own failure to anticipate them.

Here we see how the conflict between two concepts of the economy take the form of an internal psychological drama which resolves itself by dint of the sufferer's reaching the *wrong* conclusion in relation to reality and the requirements of capital. He had, however, reached the right conclusion in relation to the irreversibility of the new orthodoxy and perhaps also in relation to his own mental health. Bill's unconscious 'decision' to continue operating on an illusion, by transforming his experience in his mind in such a way as to make it correspond with his own powerful conviction, succeeded in preserving his sense of self but at the expense of shutting himself off from an important reality.

Bill's blindness to the contradiction that surrounded him is one important component contributing to the fiction that the new ideals correspond with established practice. The intentional mis-statements of the project managers, implying they can accurately assess the cost of future risk, and their silence in face of what they hold to be blatantly irrational processes, also contribute to the fictional consensus that conceals the rupture in the investment principle and cuts shareholders off from the indeterminate world that is the source of risk and of profit.

I cannot say whether executives in charge of the holding company believe that the processes they were insisting on measured risk effectively. In other companies in which I carried out fieldwork, I found that it did not necessarily follow that, because executives felt they had no alternative but to conceal risk from credit analysts; they understood the difficulties that the same demands were creating for their line management. In more than one company, my view was that executives operated on a double standard, expecting from line management what they themselves could not deliver.

This question to one side, I can say that, on the basis of what the directors of the holding company were formally being told, they had every reason to believe that the introduction of the risk assessment processes, combined with the cuts in labour, had radically reduced inefficiences without producing any adverse effects. This view, however, would be very far from the reality:

> The whole company is in denial. No one is looking at whether we are destroying our most valuable asset [the project managers]. The new vulnerabilities are not reported up. They are simply not reported.
> (Financial controller, HTDS)

From the point of view of the holding company, HTDS' success had signalled to credit rating agencies and the shareholder community that they were using their investment capital efficiently. But, in reality, the dual necessity of increasing earnings growth while simultaneously ensuring a 'safe' investment environment has introduced new vulnerabilities into the working environment which have increased uncertainties and the risk to shareholder capital. From the vantage point of credit analysts, if the subsidiary begins to fail, the conclusion is likely to be drawn that this was due to bad management – which is true. But they would be unlikely to be able to imagine that this failure of management had resulted from the investment principles on which they themselves are insisting. And while the collapse of HTDS would have a significant negative impact on the holding company and on those who depend on the company for their jobs, its impact on the industry would be negligible. A number of companies compete for its client list.

There are two myths at work here: that risk exposure can be accurately identified, and that unidentifiable risk is necessarily a threat to profit. Through their commitment to these two principles, shareholders have unintentionally shut themselves off from rational assessments of the relationship between future earnings and future loss – the opposite of the intended aim.

GLOBAL Corporation – A Major Player

The second company is seen by analysts as a global major player. It maintains year-on-year double-digit growth. In contrast with HTDS, this industrial giant controls market share for one of its three products.

From senior executives of the holding company down to supervisors of the smallest of its almost 2,000 subsidiaries, managers have a sense of the commanding position of the corporation within the overarching system; it is common knowledge that the global economy cannot function without its products and this knowledge lies at the heart of an unquestioning confidence in this company's future. External conditions do not threaten job security and each new success consolidates the sense of invulnerability. Notwithstanding its strength as a publicly listed company, GLOBAL depends on its high investment grade rating for its freedom of access to capital at preferential rates and the confidence of the international shareholder community. In light of this, I asked the CEO if the ratings were affecting the way he does business. He smiled: 'The idea is a bit ridiculous.'

Even so, between the corporation's dependence on the rating and the fact that the assessment criteria do not affect the way it does business, lies an entire infrastructure of fabrication. In contrast to HTDS, the message from the top was clear: the new orthodoxy may have created a fresh set of constraints to which the company has had to adjust, but they carry no legitimacy. As the CEO explained:

> They're not going to affect our decisions because our way of managing is entrenched, strong and effective.

This lack of ambiguity at the top is reflected all the way down the hierarchy of this vast corporation. The separation between the version of the company intended for the consumption of shareholders and credit analysts, and the principles on which the business operates, is clear to everyone. The position of the internal auditors is crucial. The six people who have legal responsibility for protecting the interests of shareholders take the view that investment principles being insisted upon by credit analysts and external auditors are not in the company's best interests. The alignment of the internal auditors with the board cannot have been a more definite statement to managers at all levels that the new ideals carry no legitimacy, and money can be invested on the basis of established criteria without fear of reprisal. At GLOBAL, there is no ambiguity about the values underpinning the formal hierarchy, and the idea that performance might one day be judged on the basis of management's ability to avoid the unexpected is nowhere in sight. Moreover there is a collective understanding that the considerable mismatch between the public face of the company and the reality is a practical necessity – an exercise in *Realpolitik*.

The burden of maintaining the public face of the company falls, in no inconsiderable measure, on the internal auditors, who are overseen by an external audit committee appointed by the board and described in the statement of accounts as established professionals who are 'tough minded and have little tolerance for breakdown in control [of risk]'. It is up to the internal auditors to reassure the external committee that risks are being properly controlled. Although the external audit committee is not a legal requirement, the board is keen to signal its willingness to shareholders to go beyond its legal obligations.

It is difficult to exaggerate the strength of the consensus organized against the new orthodoxy. But the important point is that this oppositional consensus does not find its roots in authority but in the daily experience of each manager:

> It's very simple, you cannot eliminate unpredictability. If investors knew the level of risk I deal with every day they would not invest in this company. (Manager, holding company)

> My company has the highest risk and makes the most profit. (Executive in one of GLOBAL's 2,000-plus subsidiaries)

The contradiction between the new expectation and reality is experienced at every level. However, in contrast to HTDS, it is in each case affirmed by the senior management, so that a shared understanding of the objective necessity of having to conceal risk underpins managers' activities. The security in their position was evident in the internal auditors' response to me. Once they understood I was not an advocate of the new orthodoxy, but wanted to understand the problems it was creating for the economy in general, and having carefully scrutinized the confidentiality agreement, they went out of their way to demonstrate the lengths to which they have to go to protect profitability.

High-risk strategies that are considered necessary to the corporation's future but that would be unacceptable to credit analysts were routinely downloaded into certain subsidiaries. The co-ordination required to keep strategic risk off the radar screens of the credit analysts depended on literally thousands of people working together to this end. It was with real pride that Jason, one of the internal auditors, asked me to sit down at his computer so that he could demonstrate the codes he used to communicate with subsidiaries and mask the fact that directives came from the holding company.[2] If a holding company owns 49 per cent of shares or less, the activities of the subsidiary are treated as separate and their liabilities are not included in the corporate accounts. Legally, the holding company cannot exercise influence over what are termed 'off balance sheet com-

---

[2] The company strives to keep ahead of analysts' methods of scrutiny. This corporation, like others in which I carried out fieldwork, has a research department dedicated to predicting analysts' demands for data and producing them.

panies'. Jason explained that in practice these companies are, in fact, under the control of the holding company. To conceal this, all but the most trivial communications took place either in code or in person. Jason insisted on sending me to one such subsidiary. He wanted me to see for myself what they have to do to hide what they hold to be legitimate risk.

I flew 2,000 miles to meet the internal auditor of a subsidiary that employs 85,000 people. Initially, the auditor was extremely reluctant to see me and kept me waiting several hours in an outside office. But eventually, after a telephone call to a director of the holding company, he agreed to explain how he helped to create the façade of compliance. During the course of the discussion, he seemed slowly to accept my reassurances that I had no interest in exposing him or the company, but it was not an easy meeting. He was, after all, providing me with evidence of fraud and risking serious reputational damage to the company. It is a testament to the extent to which he and others see 'façading' as a necessary consequence of a contradiction in the system, a consequence of a new and highly regressive orthodoxy, that he and others were willing to risk discussing it with me. This auditor spent two hours comparing the reality with the fiction that is sent to the internal auditors at Head Office. At the end of the discussion he offered to take me to one of the factories, over 500 miles away, but my budget would not stretch to it.[3]

In the context of this highly cohesive oppositional culture, the risk manager was hard at work. Frank had the

---

[3] Being wholly funded by the university was, in my view, critical to management's acceptance of my impartiality.

same brief as his counterpart in HTDS: to develop and implement risk assessment processes. But, unlike Bill, he had a substantial budget which he used routinely to invite top consultants into the company to advise and host workshops. During my fieldwork, it was the turn of Price Waterhouse Coopers to run a series of workshops for the corporation's most senior managers. Frank's efforts brought reward. GLOBAL Corporation was put forward as a model company – it was placed in the top 10 per cent of companies worldwide that comply with international standards of risk management.

However, in contrast to HTDS, and seemingly unbeknown to Frank, both he and his risk assessment procedures were widely acknowledged within the company to be a necessary inconvenience. The fact that he did not apparently grasp this worked in management's favour, giving the impression that he had been carefully chosen. One executive said:

These people are not high up on the IQ chart.

I spent hours in conversation with Frank. He did seem genuinely to believe in the effectiveness of his risk assessments and was keen that I should understand and share his view. On one occasion he complained to me about a director who had made it clear to him that he thought most of the questions on the seven-page risk assessment form were a waste of time. The form asked heads of divisions to identify, among other things, the potential negative impact of NGOs, new interpretations of labour legislation and new precedents set by the courts, the consequences of global strategies for Third World subsidiaries, inadequate understanding of local culture and conditions, and the stated philosophy of socialism and redistribution of wealth from the strongest trade unions. Frank felt that this director was simply not willing to make an effort. I asked him if he really thought these were reasonable questions to be asking a senior manager who did not have the benefit of a research department at his disposal. He thought about it for a moment and then said, 'Shareholders have to be able to sleep at night.'

It was extraordinary to see Frank working with such conscientious conviction, oblivious to his actual role within the company as one component in a highly elaborate programme designed to withstand the adverse affects of a misguided orthodoxy. He had been in the job for four years, so it is reasonable to assume that a temperamental characteristic partially accounted for his naivety. Having spent time with him, I think this was a key element. But managers also had a collective interest in ensuring that he was not disabused. His naivety played into their hands. Cast as the village idiot, he was humoured and never taken seriously. Yet, at the same time, he protected managers from an orthodoxy which they believed would undermine profitability.

I have described here some of the ways in which the conflict between the new expectations and the material exigencies of productive processes work themselves out in two companies. This conflict will take different forms depending on the specific circumstances in which a company is operating, but it is clear from these examples that the contingent moral economy is not something that is just going to fade away. It may now be submerged under a new orthodoxy that takes its own premises to be universal, and it may not exist in the minds of those who are committed to the rationalist moral economy, but this does not add up to a material erasure of the contingent interpretive framework.

For those for whom the contingent moral economy defines legitimate principles of capital accumulation and expansion, the miracle that allows financial gain to win over loss – the capacity to react rationally to the unexpected – follows from the objective conditions of profit creation and cannot be changed. From their perspective, analysts can go on demanding that executives eliminate unpredictable loss until they are blue in the face, but, as long as they refuse to accept that unexpected loss is intrinsic to profit, their demands will only succeed in heightening the internal contradiction.

Towards the end of my fieldwork in the rating agencies I attempted to say as much to analysts, but each time the analysts I spoke to were absolutely closed to any such idea. 'It's not like that', was one analyst's reply, and he got up and left the room. Two analysts replied with a question: did I know of any techniques that would help them to catch executives who lie (their term)? I said that I didn't. I did, however, confirm their suspicions in an attempt to raise a question in their minds as to the possibility of *legitimate* opposition to the criteria. But there was no response to this and no interest in pursuing the discussion.

One of the truly extraordinary things revealed by the fieldwork is the force with which the values underpinning analysts' judgements protect the idea of a single, universal and fixed investment principle irrevocably tied to capitalism's past success. As I have described in chapters 3 and 4, institutional values that define the objectives of the rating agencies do not permit analysts to perceive the realities that would shatter the illusion of a continuity of the investment principle. This blindness would appear to be an important attribute of the force with which the new values are being imposed. The effect is twofold. On the one hand it has instituted a conflict that is interminably reproduced across the globe through millions of economic settings. From the perspective of the individual corporation, the shift in investors' values has changed the structure of the dynamic between investors and the corporations they own, but it has not succeeded in overturning the internal logic of the capitalist economy. On the other hand, taken from the perspective of the rating agencies – if not the conscious perspective of analysts – the clash is about redirecting the flow of capital to favour consolidation over and above competition. The salient analytic point is that both the premise of universality and the force of its conviction are misplaced and, more critically, are indifferent to the possibility of alternative perspectives.

6

Threat

Several analysts asked to speak to me off the record. They were, without exception, critical of the methodology used by the agencies to measure risk and concerned that systemic, inaccurate predictions serve to increase risk and undermine stability. Discussions with all three of the analysts cited below took place before the 2007 subprime crisis.[1] They all predicted economic collapse and, in light of the 2008 financial crisis, it does indeed look as if their prediction follows from their capacity to stand outside the rationalist framework and to take an independent stance.

Charles, New York and Paris

Charles was an acknowledged high flier. Although he had been working for the agency for only eighteen months, he was already highly regarded, which

---

[1] These included two credit analysts and one financial analyst from the banking sector.

is perhaps why two analysts independently suggested I speak to him. Our short meeting in New York was taken up with his questions about my research. This was the only time any analyst asked me to expand on my own work. Was I, he asked, trying to understand the culture of credit analysts? I said I wanted to understand the reason for the tremendous hostility towards them. He raised his eyebrows but said nothing. A month later he telephoned to say he would be in Paris the following week where he would have more time to discuss the issue I had raised.

In Paris, his tight schedule left time for a six o'clock supper. He spoke at great speed with a real sense of urgency. I have reproduced my notes verbatim to capture his sense of near panic about an impending economic collapse. The unfinished sentences reflect the difficulty I had in keeping pace.

> The by-product of what we are doing is chaos, with *no* one responsible for that chaos. The system is based on endless expansion which means players are getting fewer and fewer – the superior size and scale of US corporations means we are buying everyone else out. Now protectionism is out the window, those who are bigger and stronger choke out the others. You reduce the players to control supply and drive up prices. This means they can *control prices*. [His emphasis]

He paused to see that I was getting the significance of this last point.

> The constant push to size is creating fragility, feeding the insatiable drive for profit, taking it to its logical conclusion, the US companies tend to be larger [. . .] the points critical

to our understanding will never appear in *The Economist*. Where have these pools of capital come from? Ask yourself.

The driving force is the race for expansion. Companies will drive up debt to increase dividends to attract investors, they become over-extended, and have to sell out to bigger players or become bankrupt. Size is the issue in all industries. You have to attract investor demand and investor demand is becoming increasingly demanding. Investors like to pool their capital – more clout, less risk.

Again, he stopped to be sure the penny had dropped.

Analysts advise executives on what to do, on how to *meet* the criteria. [Company] accountants offer the same advice. Do these criteria really tell them what they need to know? In no sense are we in control. The criteria are *supposed* to be a system of standardization which overcomes all this.

Then, sarcastically:

I don't think so.
New mergers happen too fast. There is no time for integration. Executives don't know what's really happening in their own companies. There is no knowledge. There is no control. Everyone feels it: a sense of vacuum at the centre. Absentee landlord [. . .] A downgrade costs so much money. There is no way they would not be going to do everything in their control to ensure a good rating. Best bluffer wins [. . .]

They [analysts] think linearly. It's emotionally very stressful for linear thinkers to have to deal with all this. The human cost to people [at the top] in these institutions as well as underneath is high. The few people making the strategic decisions are under phenomenal stress. There is phenomenal stress on the people in there. They're [like] drowning men.

There's endless merging. Often a company gets down-graded after they merge. It costs money to buy another company. You have to borrow to buy so you have to service your debt, downsize, etc. But it's worth it to a company to have better dividends. Read *The Economist*. This is what it advocates. Read the *Wall Street Journal*.

The oligarchs of the financial institutions are the people who call the shots. No one else can compete with the size of US banks. Economies of scale make everything more controllable.

Charles went on to tell me how endless expansion and the demand for ever higher earnings growth were forcing companies to neglect environmental damage and to lie about it. It is simply not possible, he said, for companies to meet all the demands being made by shareholders and environmental groups and to make the huge investments required to protect the environment.

The only thing that makes these people sit up is a bill. Environmental factors should be included in the ratings criteria [but] it would mean fewer returns on the market than we have become used to.

Thirty years dominant in terms of corporate analysis and now they've gone from dominating the US to dominating Europe. No one can continue the kind of profit that people are expected to produce. Do you think these guys [credit analysts] invest in the market? Of course not. They invest in real estate, office blocks in Manhattan, in gold – they keep gold bars under their beds. The fragility . . .

I interrupted him: 'But they are controlling prices.'

He made no reply. He seemed to have run out of steam. I asked if many of his colleagues shared his views. 'No', was his abrupt reply.

Charles believes strongly that the ratings are a source of instability in the economy and that the criteria, far from being able to guarantee a safe investment environment, create new vulnerabilities. Notwithstanding the 2008 banking crisis and the near collapse of that sector, however, there is a real question as to whether his analysis of a radical disconnection between the criteria and reality derives from perception and understanding of the realities that face the credit rating agencies, or whether his pessimistic forecast is simply the negative version of the same universalist, rationalist principle that appears to drive other analysts.

Frank, New York

Frank is retired. Only at the end of a long discussion did he decide to tell me what he actually thought.

> Frank: Each investor is measuring against a standard that makes him feel confident. The assumption is that liquidity will handle all this – it's a house of cards no matter how you look at it. In terms of true risk management no one has a handle on how to deal with it. There is risk exposure all over the place and no one will know until it blows. Bad as they were, things were a hundred times better years ago. Now there is a false sense that risk has been reduced.
>
> Me: Other people are presumably as aware as you.
>
> Frank: No they're not. If you do point out there is a problem, if you do say the emperor has no clothes, you are

shaming them because there is no solution. It's a fictional system – a system that gets away with its consequences. The enemy is the system. The system exports poverty all over the world. It penetrates and corrupts everything, it carries disdain for everything. If you read *The Economist* there are lots of problems. But they are all good problems, they all have solutions.

Maurice, Paris

This was our first meeting. The topic was supposed to be the effect of sovereign risk on international investment strategies. Maurice seemed a little distracted. Apropos of nothing he began with a long anecdote which was not really to the point, to do with an Ambassador in Washington on the telephone to the US treasurer fixing the interest rate. I lost track of his story.

> Then they discuss what they will tell the press – 'the gimmick'. That's what they call the 'news' they feed to the press. [. . .] I spent last week on a course at Harvard Business School. One of the sessions was on venture capitalism: 'How to take the *risk* out of venture capitalism'.

He saw me smile and continued:

> The banks have discovered that the poor are honest, they pay back their debts. Which means it's good business to lend them money even without collateral.

This 'new paradigm', he said with heavy irony, had been the subject of the Harvard workshop. He went to his book shelves and took out part of the programme list. 'Day One', he read out loud, 'Ethics'. He took the cover page and pinned it on his bulletin board. Then he sat back down and looked at the page and then at me. I said I would be interested to read the chapter on ethics. He called in his secretary and asked her to photocopy the whole course.

Look at what they're doing in Tobago . . . [ironically] *creating* opportunity.

He suggested we go into the coffee room. At the end of the corridor was an elegant bar. He closed the door, offered me a chair at a table at the far end of the room and began quite spontaneously:

It is madness what is happening here. At some point it's all going to collapse. I have to say, I'm prepared. I bought a piece of land with good soil, in a warm country where I can grow tomatoes. When everything goes to hell I'll take my wife and child and leave. What they are doing is terrifying. This precision analysis . . . We are like X_1, 17. bombers. We see only what's on the radar screen. We don't know what the hell we're destroying down there. The only real question is how will we rebuild society? You're an anthropologist. . . .

I ignored this and asked him what he thought, exactly, was leading to the crisis. He did not reply so I asked if he felt anything could be done to avert it.

No, it's gone too far. And do you imagine the others are investing in the market? Of course not. Like me, they invest in land, in gold.

I asked why he didn't leave the company:

I would never be able to earn this salary. I would have to move to another part of the city, my child would have to change schools. Under these circumstances, my wife would probably divorce me. . .

He paused there, then asked me again:

But how are we to build a new society? Where are the models? Where do we begin?

The conversation went on for quite some time. Several times I tried to get him to be more specific about the causes of the forthcoming crisis but he seemed only to want to discuss what life would be like after the apocalypse. This instant openness, which at first I could not explain, made much more sense when, several weeks later, I learned he had resigned.

All three analysts are deeply fearful of the consequences of their own activity, which they see as essentially destructive. For them, the principles determining their activity produce fragility which will result – or, in Frank's view, has already resulted – in the failure of the capitalist system.

Charles sees the critical issue as the pressure inherent in the criteria towards the creation of larger and larger economic units: this is the source of instability that will ultimately lead to the collapse of capitalism. Maurice and Frank are less specific about the causes of instability but are very clear as to the outcome. For all three, the investment criteria are identified with blind and irrational forces that pose a threat to the entire social edifice that is the capitalist system. The world they conjure up is frightening indeed, not merely because it is deeply irrational, but because failure of the system appears inevitable.

On the face of it, their views appear to be entirely

discrepant with those of their colleagues who accept the official institutional line. For the three dissenters, reason has not, after all, succeeded in overcoming the obstacles to progress, and their rejection of a positive outcome appears to place them squarely outside the rationalist framework.

If, however, we examine the terms of their critique more closely, it becomes apparent that the critique is itself made from a rationalist point of view. All three dissenters are at one with their more optimistic colleagues in defining immeasurable risk as an inherent threat to the capitalist system. What cannot be seen cannot be measured, and what cannot be measured consitutes threat. That is to say, the opposition between reason and chaos is already there in the configuration of the rationalist model that defines the alternatives; the only alternative to continuing along current lines is freefall into chaos.

We see, then, that the critics too, just like those who continue to have faith in the progressive thrust of the investment criteria, are at the mercy of an evaluative framework that severely limits their choices of interpretation.[2]

---

[2] These critical analysts illustrate well the error of deducing the nature of the commitment to institutional values from conforming behaviour. We cannot know just how many analysts actually believe in the effectiveness of institutional aims. The three quoted above claim to be unique in understanding the destructive power of the agencies, yet they also say that their colleagues are investing in land and in gold, which would suggest they too have little confidence in the value of their activities. This raises the disconcerting possibility that a majority of analysts lack faith in institutional objectives. From the point of view of the overarching dynamic, however, their critical stance and their moral discomfort with the effects of their own activity is irrelevant. Irrespective of whether analysts' motives originate in voluntary acceptance or external constraint, what counts in terms of preserving the present dynamic is the willingness to act on behalf of institutional principles.

It is important to emphasize that it does not follow from this that individuals operating within the rationalist framework cannot, under any circumstances, question its presuppositions and change their way of thinking. Although, arguably, history is mainly a record of social groups and classes that have failed to examine their own deeply inculcated habits of thought, we cannot in fact know under what conditions people might apperceive the assumptions that up until that moment have co-ordinated their interests and ambitions. What this analysis shows, however, is just how easily the rationalist model incorporates a critical and 'independent' attitude, creating the illusion that it is being seen 'objectively' from the outside.

Both the pessimists and the optimists are united, however, by the same cognitive proposition. For both, the kind of reason that makes progress possible carries an absolute value. When this reason fails, the world falls apart.

As I describe in chapter 3, the assumptions underlying the evaluative framework that takes reason (in a specific and narrow sense) to be universal are deeply rooted in western society and culture and backed by some of history's greatest intellectual authorities. This in itself goes a long way to explaining the tenacity of the rationalist model. However, to leave the argument here would do nothing to dispel the idea that those who see the world through the prism of the rationalist framework would respond rationally to strong evidence or powerful argument that demonstrates the framework's foundational premises to be unsound.

The ethnography presented here strongly suggests that this is not the case. The universalist concept of reason, which, as we have seen, involves many conceptualizations, perceptual experiences and assumptions about the laws of nature, rules out the possibility of an alternative standpoint. It is not just a matter of those committed to the rationalist model having no independent point of leverage to raise their interpretive schema into a relative representation, but of this particular schema not allowing for the possibility of an alternative conception of independent reality. This point is vital because it means that those for whom the rationalist model determines coherence and defines 'real' economic relations cannot escape their confinement to its limits. Even a deep scepticism about the link between reason and progress and an ever-present fear are not enough to illuminate the relation between the universal principles that for them define the economy and the reality that these principles exclude.

The most significant bit of reality being excluded here is that the reason and concomitant values analysts hold to be universal break with established principles of capital accumulation and expansion. As I describe in chapter 2, the fiction of continuity that follows from their inability to grasp this fact masks the discontinuity between past and present, making it extremely difficult to assess the impact of what is in fact an entirely new set of ideals. Comparing the two perspectives has provided some insight into the nature of these ideals and their viability as a rational force.

From the perspective of what I have called the 'contingent model', immeasurable risk is seen as intrinsic to the process of wealth creation. From this other standpoint, investors' preoccupation with predictive accuracy appears to *follow from* a new identification of immeasurable risk with threat. One might even go so far as to argue that it is an irrational fear of chaos and the collapse of the capitalist system that lies behind an exaggerated faith in the mathematical and statistical techniques used to model and cost risk.

The alarming implication is that those men and women who perceive the economy through the prism of the rationalist framework may at once be aware that the assessment techniques do not accurately cost risk (as in the case of the critics quoted above) and be incapable of questioning the premises that led them to accept the validity of the investment crieria in the first place.[3]

Given the widely held view among policy-makers that the failure to cost risk accurately is a major cause of the 2008 banking crisis, a pressing question is whether the rationalist framework is determining the analysis of the causes of the systemic underpricing of risk. White House policy-makers are unanimous in their judgement that it is in the assessment of risk that the financial system failed. The public position, at least, is that banks and other institutional investors adopted a reckless attitude towards investment and abandoned their

[3] In a bizarre twist, Edmund Phelps, the Nobel Prize-winner for Economics in 2006, appears to be introducing a rationalist interpretation of Knightian uncertainty. Wih reference to the 2008 crisis, he says that investors 'had no sense of the existing Knightian uncertainty. So they had no sense of the possibility of a huge break in housing prices and no sense of the fundamental inapplicability of the risk management models used in the banks. . . . The volatility of the price [of risk] as it vibrates around some path was considered but not the uncertainty of the path itself: the risk that it would *shift down*' (my emphasis). Phelps continues to identify risk with threat where Frank Knight is firmly in the camp of the contingent moral economy and sees unmeasurable risk as intrinsic to a healthy market dynamic. 'Uncertainty Bedevils the Best Systems', *Financial Times*, 14 April 2009.

responsibility to limit immeasurable risk and keep to safe strategic pursuits. According to this view, an apparently uncontrollable desire to take ever greater risks with borrowed money ultimately increased uncertainty and undermined stability.

This apparent reluctance to control risk was further compounded by the capricious practices of all three major credit rating agencies to which responsibility for assessing and keeping abreast of risk exposure had been delegated. The three agencies are being targeted and held to account for distortions in the ratings which gave investment grades to banks on the brink of financial collapse. Here, too, the systemic underpricing of risk is being explained in terms of irresponsible behaviour, in this case a conflict of interest between the companies who pay for the ratings and the agencies who make the evaluations. But whether an intentional masking of risk by analysts was a significant factor in precipitating the banking crisis, or a factor at all, the focus on irresponsibility serves to deflect attention from the more important question: namely, does this hypothesis of irresponsibility follow from an evaluative framework that does not permit the accuracy of the risk assessment models to be openly challenged?

If the consequence of failed calculations is the collapse of the system, the very question of the accuracy of the risk modelling techniques raises the spectre of an impending defeat over which they could have no control. And if the possibility of the failure of the models to price risk accurately affords a perpetual threat to the economy's existence, then it follows that policy-makers would be driven to define the problem in terms that appear to offer a solution: bad behaviour, they assume, can be corrected.

It follows from this that even those policy-makers who may be privately questioning the accuracy of the assessment methods would be unable, or unwilling, to admit openly to the possibility that the models have failed, because, from within the terms of the rationalist framework, such an admission would leave them defenceless against an impending chaos that would threaten to destroy the economic order. For those able to question the investment criteria, the problem would appear intractable and, because of this, we cannot accuse them of a moral failure. From their perspective, they are simply caught up in a set of deep contradictions over which they have no control.

The important point here is that policy-makers' assessment of the causes of the crisis and the nature of the threat to the economy does appear to be a function of the internal logic of an evaluative framework whose relation to reality is deeply flawed.

The point of disconnection from reality – the unquestionable and self-validating identification of immeasurable risk with threat – leads to the frightening prospect that faith in the accuracy of the calculations, now powerfully instituted in the economy, is both irrational and irreversible.

But when we look at this same phenomenon from a different perspective – that of the corporations, in particular the major players – this frightening conclusion is an obvious product of the rationalist mindset. From this other angle, the identification of risk with threat does not in itself pose a danger to the capitalist dynamic. On the contrary, as I describe in chapter 2, the limitations lurking in specious universal principles are a powerful instrument in the service of strengthening the underlying conditions of capitalism's success. Standing with the global major players, it is clear that the internal shift in investors' values is at once a source of conflict and, by virtue of investors' conviction that control of market share guarantees the measurable uncertainty they are looking for, serves to privilege economic activity that favours capital consolidation. It is at this point, where investors' values meet the consolidating demands of major players, that the two universes work in tandem.

It is in the context of the reorientation of the underlying conditions of capitalism that we see the temporal continuity and whole topography of a transformation from one form of capital accumulation and expansion to another. From this standpoint the conflict between two concepts of productive capital, and perhaps even the crises we have recently been witnessing, are merely symptoms of a much deeper economic transformation towards a dynamic that privileges capital consolidation over and above market competition. The fact that investors' new-found dependency on accurate calculation serves to reorientate the conditions of capitalism's stability is not a choice of consciousness, but of history. How this history has come to give greater positive value to capital consolidation is a question we shall have to leave to historians.

References

Calder, A. 2008. *Corporate Governance: A Practical Guide to the Legal Frameworks and International Codes of Practice*, London and Philadelphia: Kogan Page.

Choudry, M. 2006. *Corporate Bond Markets: Instruments and Applications*, Singapore: John Wiley & Sons.

Gorton, G. and Metrick, A. 2009. 'Securitized Banking and the Run on the Repo'. Yale University ICF Working Paper no. 09–14.

Ho, K. 2009. *Liquidated, An Ethnography of Wall Street*, Durham and London: Duke University Press.

Jensen, M. and Meckling, W. 1976. 'Theory of the Firm: Managerial Behavior, Agency Costs and Ownership Structure'. *Journal of Financial Economics* 3(4): 305–60.

Knight, F. 1921. *Risk, Uncertainty and Profit*, New York: Houghton Mifflin.

Navaretti, G. and Venables, A. 2004. *Multinational Firms in the World Economy*, Princeton: Princeton University Press.

Newman, P., Millgate, M. and Eatwell, J. (eds.) 1992. *The New Palgrave Dictionary of Money & Finance*, New York and London: Macmillan.

Parry, J. and Bloch, M. (eds.) 1989. 'Introduction: Money and the Morality of Exchange'. In *Money and the Morality of Exchange*, pp. 1–32, Cambridge: Cambridge University Press.

Smith, A. 1976. *An Inquiry into the Nature and Causes of the Wealth of Nations*, Oxford: Oxford University Press.

Tett, G. 2009. *Fool's Gold: How Unrestrained Greed Corrupted a Dream, Shattered Global Markets and Unleashed a Catastrophe*, London: Little, Brown.

Toren, C. 1999. *Mind, Materiality and History*, London: Routlcdge.

Index

Index

Index

Keynes, John Maynard, 30
Knight, Frank, 30n10, 122n3

labour cuts, 90
legislation, 11, 14n1, 24–5, 91
Lehman Brothers, 3, 11
liquid assets, 15
London Stock Exchange, 2,
    5n3, 13
loss
    assumption of executive
        irresponsibility, 67
    control over, 17, 18
    credit analysts' methods,
        40–1
    HTDS, 92–3, 95, 97, 98–100
    innovation and, 6
    knowability, 21, 23
    possibility of, 86
    profit and, 18–19, 48, 50,
        109
    unpredictability mistakenly
        identified with, 63
    see also risk

managers
    response to uncertainty,
        85–6
    risk assessment workshop,
        94–8, 100
    see also executives
manufacturing industry, 84–5
market economy, 47n6
Marx, Karl, 27
mathematics, 67, 68
mergers and acquisitions, 44n5,
    113, 114
Merrill Lynch, 72
modelling, 10, 12, 39–40
monopoly, 47n6
Moody's, 3, 37n2, 47n6

moral economy, 29–30
    contingent, 70n7, 76, 108–9,
        122n3
    rationalist, 69, 71, 75, 108–9
moral failure, 10
moral issues, 27–8, 66
    see also ethics

naivety, 23–4, 108
negligence, 12n9
negotiation, 56
nervous breakdown of risk
    manager, 98–9
neutrality, 63, 64, 67, 69, 75,
    78
New York Stock Exchange, 5n3

'off balance sheet companies',
    105–6
oil industry, 83–4
oppositional culture, 104,
    106–7

Pennsylvania & Central
    Railway Company, 35–6,
    37
performance measurement,
    93–4, 96–7
Phelps, Edmund, 122n3
planning, 92, 93
pragmatic approach, 77, 97
prediction, 17, 42–3, 49–51,
    54, 111
prices, 112, 114
PricewaterhouseCoopers, 107
profit, 28–9, 65
    contingent model, 20
    loss and, 18–19, 48, 50,
        109
    risk as condition of, 2, 17–18,
        30n10, 102

Index